America's Black Founders

Revolutionary Heroes and Early Leaders

★ ★ ★

WITH 21 ACTIVITIES

Nancy I. Sanders

CHICAGO
REVIEW
PRESS

Library of Congress Cataloging-in-Publication Data

Sanders, Nancy I.
  America's Black founders : revolutionary heroes and early leaders with 21 activities / Nancy I. Sanders.
       p. cm.
  Includes bibliographical references.
  ISBN 978-1-55652-811-8 (pbk.)
  1. African American leadership—History—18th century—Juvenile literature.
  2. African American leadership—History—18th century—Study and teaching—programs—Juvenile literature. 3. African American leadership—History—19th century—Juvenile literature. 4. African American leadership—History—19th century—Study and teaching—Activity programs—Juvenile literature. 5. African Americans—History—Juvenile literature. 6. African Americans—History—Study and teaching—Activity programs—Juvenile literature. I. Title.

  E185.18.S265 2010
  973'.0496073—dc22

  2009025696

Cover and interior design: Sarah Olson
Front cover images used courtesy of the following: Richard Allen, Mother Bethel AME Church, photography by E. B.
    Lewis; Peter Williams and Jarena Lee, Library Company of Philadelphia; Crispus Attucks, Library of Congress.
Back cover images used courtesy of the following: Sarah Allen, Mother Bethel AME Church, photography by E. B.
    Lewis; William Lee, Library of Congress; Frank Johnson, New York Public Library.

Published by Chicago Review Press, Incorporated
814 North Franklin Street
Chicago, Illinois 60610
ISBN 978-1-55652-811-8
Printed in the United States of America
5 4 3 2 1

For Jeff, and all the wonderful students in Mr. Sanders's fourth grade class at Fairmont Elementary.

God bless our native land,
Her homes and children bless,
Oh may she ever stand
For truth and righteousness.

— From "God Bless Our Native Land"
by Frances Ellen Watkins Harper

Contents

Time Line

1760 Briton Hammon publishes the first African American autobiography

1770 Crispus Attucks dies in the Boston Massacre as the first martyr of the American Revolution

1773 Phillis Wheatley publishes *Poems on Various Subjects, Religious and Moral*

1775 Prince Hall founds African Lodge No. 1 in Boston
Minuteman Prince Estabrook fights at Lexington
Minuteman Peter Salem fights at Concord
Lemuel Haynes writes the ballad *The Battle of Lexington*
Petition submitted to honor Salem Poor's bravery at the Battle of Bunker Hill

1776 James Forten hears the first public reading of the Declaration of Independence

1778 Nero Hawley earns exemplary pay at Valley Forge

The First Rhode Island Regiment fights bravely at Yorktown 1781
in the last battle of the Revolutionary War

Richard Allen and Absalom Jones found the Free African Society in Philadelphia 1787

Prince Hall petitions for safe return of kidnapped free blacks sold into slavery, and wins 1788

John Marrant delivers his popular sermon as chaplain of Prince Hall's African Lodge of Masons 1789

Philadelphia, the nation's largest population of free blacks, becomes the temporary capital of the United States 1790

Benjamin Banneker is appointed to help survey Washington, D.C. 1791

Benjamin Banneker publishes his first almanac 1792

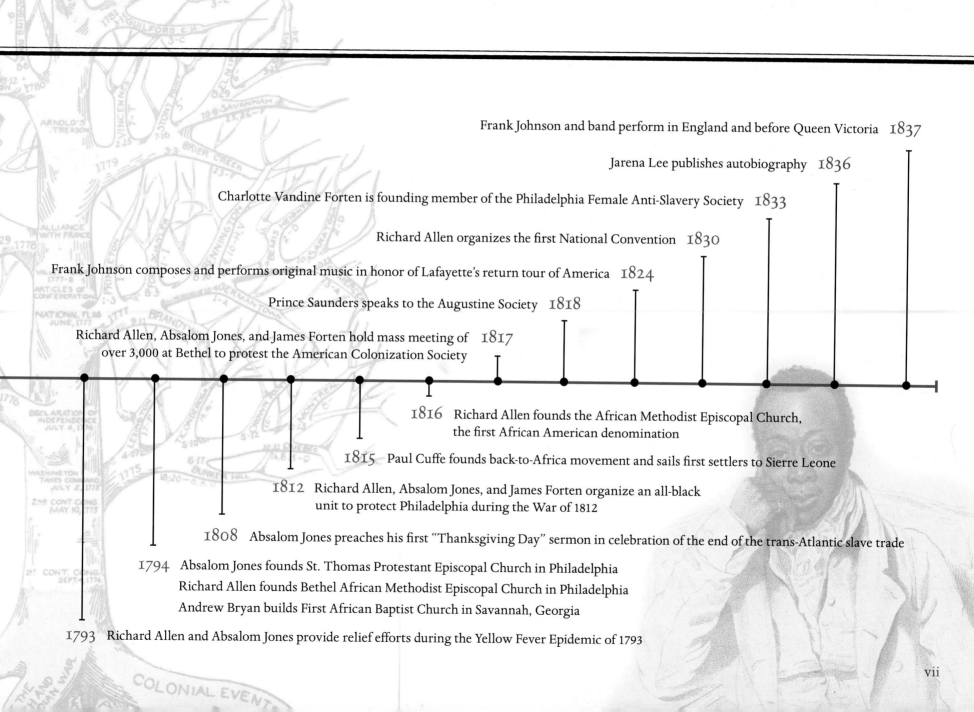

Frank Johnson and band perform in England and before Queen Victoria 1837

Jarena Lee publishes autobiography 1836

Charlotte Vandine Forten is founding member of the Philadelphia Female Anti-Slavery Society 1833

Richard Allen organizes the first National Convention 1830

Frank Johnson composes and performs original music in honor of Lafayette's return tour of America 1824

Prince Saunders speaks to the Augustine Society 1818

Richard Allen, Absalom Jones, and James Forten hold mass meeting of 1817
over 3,000 at Bethel to protest the American Colonization Society

1816 Richard Allen founds the African Methodist Episcopal Church,
the first African American denomination

1815 Paul Cuffe founds back-to-Africa movement and sails first settlers to Sierre Leone

1812 Richard Allen, Absalom Jones, and James Forten organize an all-black
unit to protect Philadelphia during the War of 1812

1808 Absalom Jones preaches his first "Thanksgiving Day" sermon in celebration of the end of the trans-Atlantic slave trade

1794 Absalom Jones founds St. Thomas Protestant Episcopal Church in Philadelphia
Richard Allen founds Bethel African Methodist Episcopal Church in Philadelphia
Andrew Bryan builds First African Baptist Church in Savannah, Georgia

1793 Richard Allen and Absalom Jones provide relief efforts during the Yellow Fever Epidemic of 1793

1ST CHURCH

2ND CHURCH

CHURCH AFRICAN

EPISCOPAL METHODIST

RICHARD ALLEN

FOUNDER
1760 - 1831

4TH CHURCH

3RD CHURCH

"When in the Course of Human Events..."

★ ★ ★

COLONIAL DAYS

In 1760, Richard Allen was born. Not noticed by the world, far away from the royal palace in England, not even affected by the talk of freedom and liberty in colonial America, the news reached the ears of his mother's master in Philadelphia, Pennsylvania: another slave had been born.

Richard's mother held him close, hoping against hope to shield her innocent baby from the harsh realities of slavery, that "peculiar institution," which supplied the rich treasures for the king and gave the colonists leisure to pursue their liberties in the New World. Yet slavery held no freedom or liberties for the slave.

As Richard's mother rocked her newborn baby to sleep, what thoughts crossed her mind? She knew too well of the slave's auction block where babies were torn from their mother's arms and sold away to a different owner, never to be seen again. Her own father, a white colonist, had sold her and her mother as if they were cattle.

As she counted her baby's 10 little fingers and 10 little toes, Richard's mother could not count on his future. It would have warmed her mother's heart, however, to know that one day her son would return to Philadelphia, the city of his birth, to become the greatest and most influential leader of free blacks in the newly formed United States of America.

He would use his freedom to fight for the liberty and justice of all African Americans—both enslaved and free. Richard Allen would lead the way. He would be the first to forge footsteps and create a path along the trail of freedom for others to follow. He would rise up from the pit of slavery to become one of the Black Founders of America.

The House of Benjamin Chew

At the time Richard Allen was born, slavery was firmly established throughout the American colonies. Allen's father first arrived in Philadelphia, Pennsylvania, on a slave ship from the Caribbean. He and his wife and children were the property of a Quaker master, Benjamin Chew.

When their son, Richard, was born on February 14, 1760, the Philadelphia household of Benjamin Chew was a hub of important political activity. Chew was climbing the political ladder in colonial America. He was appointed the attorney general of the Province of Pennsylvania from 1755 to 1769. By the time Richard Allen was toddling around his mother's skirts, Benjamin Chew lived in an elegant house of the fashionable neighborhood on South Third Street in Philadelphia.

> "Slavery is a bitter pill."
> —Richard Allen

Benjamin Chew was a friend of George Washington and John Adams. Pennsylvania's famous Penn family hired his law services. However, Chew disagreed with the political stance of Benjamin Franklin. Chew did not support the signing of the Declaration of Independence. During his early years in the Chew household, Richard Allen probably saw important political figures, helped prepare for the flurry of political activities, and overheard heated discussions.

In 1767, there were nearly 1,400 slaves living in the city of Philadelphia. This meant that about one out of every five households owned slaves. Benjamin Chew's large family of 10 usually had about 12 workers in their home at any given time. These workers were paid employees, indentured servants, or slaves.

These workers probably kept out of sight. Breakfast was cooked and the table prepared while the Chew family dressed in their bedrooms. When the family came in to eat, the workers went to the bedrooms to tidy the rooms.

Positions at the household usually included a coachman, maids and menservants, a cook, a washerwoman, and a nurse for the children. Younger slaves, such as Richard, helped out in any way they could. There were always jobs such as carrying wood for the fireplace, stuffing straw in a mattress, or helping the sons and daughters of Benjamin Chew.

The Slave Mother

BY FRANCES ELLEN WATKINS HARPER

Heard you that shriek? It rose
So wildly on the air,
It seemed as if a burdened heart
Was breaking in despair.
Saw you those hands so sadly clasped—
The bowed and feeble head—
The shuddering of that fragile form—
That look of grief and dread?
Saw you the sad, imploring eye?
Its every glance was pain,
As if a storm of agony
Were sweeping through the brain.
She is a mother pale with fear,
Her boy clings to her side,
And in her kyrtle* vainly tries
His trembling form to hide.
He is not hers, although she bore
For him a mother's pains;
He is not hers, although her blood
Is coursing through his veins!

A kyrtle is a woman's long skirt or dress.

He is not hers, for cruel hands
May rudely tear apart
The only wreath of household love
That binds her breaking heart.
His love has been a joyous light
That over her pathway smiled,
A fountain gushing ever new,
Amid life's desert wild.
His lightest word has been a tone
Of music round her heart,

Their lives a streamlet blent in one—
Oh, Father! must they part?
They tear him from her circling arms,
Her last and fond embrace.
Oh! never more may her sad eyes
Gaze on his mournful face.
No marvel, then, these bitter shrieks
Disturb the listening air;
She is a mother, and her heart
Is breaking in despair.

A slave auction.
Courtesy of the Library of Congress, Prints & Photographs Division, LC-USZ62-2582

A Summer Home

When Richard Allen was two years old, a yellow fever epidemic swept through the city of Philadelphia. Dr. Benjamin Rush, a local doctor, described the terrors of 1762 in his papers. As an active physician in the city, he documented as many as 20 deaths a day from August through December. When the fever was over, about one-sixth of Philadelphia's population had died.

This horrible outbreak of yellow fever probably prompted Benjamin Chew to purchase land in Germantown, six miles from Philadelphia. For the next four years he built a summer home called Cliveden on this plot with plans of moving his family away from the city to stay there during the hottest months each year.

Cliveden was expensive to build. Chew's records show he paid large sums of money to build this majestic mansion. By 1767, with the completion of Cliveden, Benjamin Chew sold some of his slaves.

> "[We] were sold into Delaware State, near Dover."
> —Richard Allen

Going . . . Going . . . Gone . . . SOLD!

Richard was only about seven years old when the normal routine of his life was uprooted. Richard Allen, his mother and father, and his brother and two sisters were sold to a farmer named Stokeley Sturgis who lived near Dover, Delaware. Richard now joined the ranks of countless other African Americans throughout the colonies who toiled in the fields.

Richard lived and worked on a plantation near Dover through the rest of his childhood. He did not have a childhood, really. He was not free to wander the countryside and play simple boyhood games. He was a slave.

So he worked. His back ached from plowing and planting and hoeing the weeds. His hands grew rough from chopping wood. His feet grew tired from standing and walking and working from sunup to sundown, and even into the darkness of night. And yet his heart grew strong. A seed of hope sprouted and grew inside, yearning to be free.

Freedom was a constant thought to this young man known to the world at this time only as Richard. Although we do not know exactly when he acquired his last name, on historical documents the name "Allen" does not appear until *after* he bought his freedom.

After Richard and his family became the property of Stokeley Sturgis, his mother had

Food and Clothing Allotment

In 1772, E. Tilghman, a relative of the Chew family, published a small pamphlet recommending a food and clothing allotment for slaves. Benjamin Chew supposedly followed this guide for his household. Even though Richard Allen was sold by the time it was printed, this document gives us a closer glimpse into what it might have been like to live and work for the Chew family.

"RULES FOR CLOATHING AND FEEDING NEGROES"
E. Tilghman (1772)

Two shirts and shifts a year of the best homespun linen to be given them at about the month of November.

A waistcoat of homespun half-fulled or white kersey [coarse, woolen cloth] for the men made like a sailor's pea jacket with strong cheap metal buttons, a patch strongly put on each elbow and shoulder; the seams to be back with double thread, stitched backwards and forwards, a pair of town trousers for the men in harvest and a short shirt to reap in, open at the bottom and to reach a little below the waistband of the breeches.

One of the above waistcoats will serve them two years giving them the second year a body jacket to come just below the waistband of the breeches loose-bodied waistcoat of very strong flannel.

Handmade replica of
sailor's pea jacket.
Courtesy of G. Calder

When the men work in the cold weather, the upper jacket should be thrown off as soon as they begin to grow warm with labour and put on again immediately upon them leaving to prevent colds, illnesses, etc.

The women to be clothed with petticoat and waistcoat made of best Welch cotton or country cloth. The jacket half-fulled, the petticoat only seamed in the common way.

Bedding:
1 rug, 2 Dutch blankets for they will lay on one and cover with the second
Mattress of straw or chaff (to be changed after childbirth)
Needles and Thread (especially darning needles to repair clothing)

1 pair shoes about the middle of November and another about the 1st of January for men. 1 pair for women about 1st December. 1 pair stronger country-made stockings in November.

6 Barrels or 30 Bushels Indian Corn—horses for 1 year.

3 Barrels or 15 Bushels—per Negro.

Courtesy of Cliveden, a National Trust Historic Site, and the Historical Society of Pennsylvania

Stuff a Straw Mattress

During the founding years of our nation, many people slept on mattresses that were stuffed with straw. Stuffing a mattress with straw was dusty, dirty work. It was a job often assigned to those who were enslaved.

You can stuff a mattress with your friends. When you're done, take turns resting on it or reading a book.

Materials

★ Dry, open area out of doors or in a barn or shed

★ Old duvet cover (or large flat sheet folded in half and sewn down the sides and across the bottom to resemble an oversized pillowcase open at one end)

★ Bale of straw

★ Broom

1. Work on a dry, open area where you can spread out the mattress on the floor or ground.

2. Grab a handful of loose straw and stuff it inside the duvet cover. Reach in as far as you can to position the straw at the bottom of the mattress.

3. Continue to stuff handfuls of straw into the duvet cover until it is almost full.

4. When done, fold over the flap of fabric at the opening so the straw stays inside.

5. Clean up the work area with a broom.

several more children. But their master was in debt, so one day Sturgis sold Richard's mother and three of his brothers and sisters. Such was the heartbreaking life of a slave.

Africans in America

The history of Africans in America traces its roots back in time to centuries before Richard Allen was born. During the Middle Ages, long before the trans-Atlantic slave trade began, kingdoms in Africa flourished as wealthy and influential powers. The glorious golden empires of Ghana, Songhay, and Mali rose and fell. Caravans arrived in famous cities throughout these magnificent kingdoms from around the known world. Scholars and artists and traders traveled to Timbuktu, that world-renowned center of learning, trade, and religion. Around 1000 A.D., seven ancient walled cities called *birane* were built in the area now known as Nigeria. These seven city-states were important posts on the sub-Saharan trade routes. Many journeyed to the ancient walled city of Kano where they sought the same magnificent indigo-dyed blue cloth that can still be found in this city in northern Nigeria today.

In the early 1300s, nearly 200 years before Columbus set foot in the Americas, Abubakari II, the wealthy king of Mali, organized two great expeditions. In his second fleet, over 2,000 ships set sail from the shores of Africa to follow the path of the setting sun across the Atlantic Ocean. The king himself sailed in the lead.

The expeditions never returned to Africa. No one knows for sure whether they ever reached the Americas. However, archaeological and historical evidence suggest that Africans arrived on these shores long before the Europeans. When Columbus, Balboa, and other Europeans arrived, they found small groups of people who appeared to be of African descent. Also, ancient Olmec stone heads have been found in the region of Mexico and Central America. Carved with distinctly African facial features, some of these stone giants stand 9 feet high and weigh 40 tons.

top: Ancient dye pits are still used in Kano today.
Courtesy of Eugene Eric Kim

bottom: Travelers still come to Kano, Nigeria, in search of their world-famous indigo-dyed blue cloth.
Courtesy of Eugene Eric Kim

Olmec stone head.
Courtesy of Amano Artisan Chocolate

Before Jamestown

Long before colonists established the first permanent settlement in the English colonies, Africans were members of the earliest exploring parties brave enough to sail across the Atlantic Ocean. Africans journeyed with Europeans to the Americas as conquistadors, mariners, explorers, settlers, and slaves.

Pedro Alonzo Niño sailed with Christopher Columbus as navigator in 1492. Conquistador Juan Garrido fought with Hernando Cortés against the Aztecs to conquer what is now known as Mexico City. Juan Valiente was a black conquistador of Chile. Juan Garcia and Miguel Ruiz were black conquistadors of Peru. Nuflo de Olano was part of Balboa's exploring party in 1513 when they first saw the Pacific Ocean. Estevanico's brave adventures led him to explore Florida. Later, he guided an overland expedition through New Mexico in his quest to find the famous "Seven Cities of Gold."

Spanish expeditions attempted to establish permanent settlements in what is now known as the United States. Both free and enslaved

> *"If you love your children, if you love your country, if you love the God of love, clear your hands from slaves."*
> —Richard Allen

Africans were members of these expeditions. In 1565, the settlement of St. Augustine, Florida, was founded. Africans, with their skills in metalworking, construction, and farming, were invaluable to the new community.

The First Africans in English Colonies

The year was 1619. The place was Jamestown, Virginia. John Rolfe and the other English colonists were struggling to survive in the harsh, dangerous wilderness. Suddenly one day a ship, the *White Lion*, appeared on the horizon. On board were Africans in chains who had been captured from a slave ship sailing from Africa to Spanish colonies much farther south in the Americas. That eventful day, about 20 Africans were sold as indentured servants to John Rolfe and the other colonists.

Antony, Isabella, and the other new arrivals were skilled farmers and metalworkers from the kingdom of Ndongo in Angola. Unlike many of the English colonists, these Angolans knew how to grow important crops for food such as yams, grains, and corn. They knew how to grow tobacco, the crop that could be sold to England for cash. Former blacksmiths in their homeland, they made iron tools and weapons. With the skill and labor of these first Angolans, the colony of

Jamestown no longer struggled to survive. And after they served their terms of contracts as indentured servants, many of these men and women earned their freedom.

The Trans-Atlantic Slave Trade

One year after the arrival of Africans in Jamestown, the *Mayflower* set sail and headed to America carrying its boatload of Pilgrims. A steady stream of English colonists began arriving by ship to settle in the wilderness and forests. By this time, the slave trade was already well established in the Caribbean and in South America.

After Columbus sailed across the Atlantic Ocean to North and South America, European countries rushed to conquer and settle the rugged, previously uncharted wilderness. Workers were needed to carve out settlements and work to harvest profits from crops. The trans-Atlantic slave trade was organized by wealthy European companies as a system to provide forced labor to meet this need. It was a dark, sad period of history that stained every individual and every nation involved.

Forts were built along the coast of Africa to hold captured Africans until enough were gathered to cram into overcrowded slave ships. Men, women, and children from all levels of education, position, and wealth were torn from their homeland. All rights and identity were stripped away from them.

The voyage across the Atlantic Ocean became known as the Middle Passage, a time of horror and death for many. Often, slave ships landed first in Brazil or the West Indies to supply workers for the huge sugar, indigo, and coffee plantations there. They then headed up the coast to stop at English colonies in North America.

At various ports, the ships were loaded with crops and raw goods. Eventually, they set sail back to England or other European countries. Back in Europe, the raw goods were manufactured into products such as guns, fabric, and rum. Ships then headed back to Africa to trade their goods for captured slaves. Finally, in the early 1800s, both Britain and the United States outlawed the trans-Atlantic slave trade. Even though slave ships were no longer permitted to bring captive Africans to America, slavery continued in the United States until 1865, when the Civil War finally brought it to an end.

Africans' Culture and Skills

According to the newly forming laws throughout the colonies, enslaved men, women, and children with an African heritage had legal and personal rights taken away from them.

Yet in the midst of an era filled with stories of deep tragedy and sorrow, individuals and groups of African Americans rose up with strength and dignity to establish a place and identity for themselves and influence the founding of America.

Many enslaved individuals brought their culture with them from Africa. They influenced America as much as it influenced them. From crafting agricultural tools that they had used successfully in their native land, to cooking favorite dishes from their homeland, to holiday celebrations, to language customs and music and dance, Africans arriving in America shaped the foundation of the new country in countless, important ways.

Toward the end of the 1700s, the city of Charleston, South Carolina, was the largest center of slavery in the newly forming nation.

"The African slave who sailed to the New World did not sail alone. People brought their culture, no matter how adverse the circumstances. And therefore part of America is African."

—Henry Louis Gates Jr.

Positioned on the Atlantic Ocean, numerous slave ships sailed into port each year. These ships were greeted by plantation owners looking for strong, healthy workers from specific regions of Africa known for their skills in growing certain crops.

Frequent ads appeared in local papers such as the *South Carolina and American General Gazette*. These ads recommended the outstanding skills of numerous enslaved artisans and laborers in various shops throughout the city. Africans now living in America provided much of the skill and labor needed to build an emerging nation.

~ Weave a Fanner ~

Baskets called fanners were used to winnow rice during harvest time. These large, flat baskets curved slightly upward at the edge. Grains of rice were piled in the basket. Holding the fanner in both hands, workers, mostly women, tossed the rice into the air, letting the breeze carry away the light chaff, or husks, covering the rice. The heavier grains of rice fell back into the fanning basket.

Beautifully crafted, hand-coiled fanners were used on rice plantations throughout South Carolina and other southern states. The origins of these baskets can be traced to Senegal where women constructed them using a tall grass grown in the region called ndone.

Adult supervision required

Materials

★ Raffia

★ Embroidery Needle (blunt-nosed with a large eye)

★ Scissors

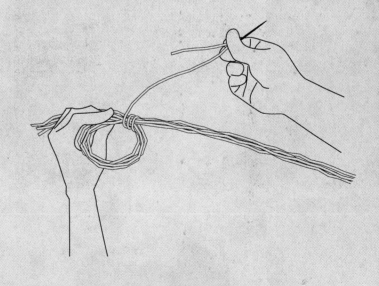

1. Thread a single piece of long, sturdy raffia through a needle.

2. Pull apart about a dozen strands of raffia and hold them in one bunch.

3. Make a small circle with one end of the bunch. Sew it together with the raffia thread by making loops around the small circle with the thread. Do not use knots as you weave your basket, but make several loops around the bunch until the end of the thread is secured.

4. Gently pull the long end of the bunch until the circle is smaller. Trim off the short ends of the bunch close to your work.

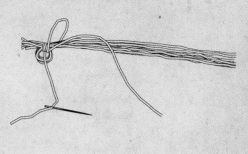

5. Carefully coil the loose bunch of raffia around the circle you made. While you do, sew loops of the raffia thread around the two coils. Try to keep the stitches of thread evenly spaced apart as you continue to sew.

6. Continue wrapping the bunch of raffia around the coil, stitching as you go.

7. Add new strands of raffia to the bunch as old strands run out. Simply place the new strands at the end of the old strands and stitch over them to hold them in place. No knots are needed.

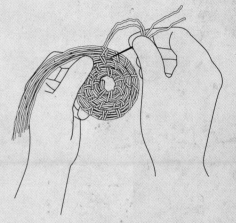

8. Try to keep the basket fairly flat as you work. Raise the edge of the basket slightly as you complete the basket by bringing the bunch of raffia up as you coil it and stitch the last few rows in place.

9. Make your basket the size that you want or just use up all the raffia. A fanner used for winnowing rice measured about two feet across. When you are done, stitch the ends of the bunch down securely and then slip the end of the thread in through the previous row of stitches. Carefully cut off the thread close to the basket.

Classic fanner basket.
Courtesy of Drayton Hall, National Trust for Historic Preservation

Winnowing the rice.
Courtesy of Drayton Hall, National Trust for Historic Preservation

Drayton Hall

Drayton Hall was one of the larger plantations near Charleston, South Carolina. This rice plantation was home to numerous enslaved people from Angola in southern Africa and Senegal in western Africa. However, slaves were not only of African descent. During early colonial days, nearly one-third of those who were enslaved in the region surrounding Charleston were Native American. Plus, a significant number of enslaved people had ancestors from both cultures—Native American and African.

Because of the skills and knowledge Africans brought with them, cultivating and harvesting rice became an important industry in America.

A Life of Adventure and Influence

Not every African American living in the South was enslaved, however. John Marrant had been born free in New York. Both his parents were free. After his father died, his mother moved with her four children deep into the southern colonies. First living in St. Augustine, Florida, then moving up to Georgia, the family eventually moved to live in Charleston, South Carolina. Marrant grew up to write and publish the story of his life in the popular book, *A Narrative of the Lord's Wonderful Dealings with John Marrant, A Black.*

Young John Marrant lived life in a big way. When he was a child, his mother held great dreams for her little son, and made certain he learned to read and write. But her plans to have him learn a useful trade disappeared

left: Drayton Hall, built circa 1738.

Courtesy of Drayton Hall, National Trust for Historic Preservation

right: Threshing rice.

Courtesy of the Library of Congress, Prints & Photographs Division, LC-USZ62-61966

when he set his heart on playing the violin and the French horn, instead. He had a passion for music. By the time he was a teenager, he had learned to play the violin and French horn so well that wealthy gentry paid him big money to entertain them. He earned large sums of money playing throughout Charleston for wealthy parties, balls, dances, and important events.

His life changed when he was 14, however. On the way to perform his French horn at a social, Marrant decided to drop in at a local meeting place where a huge crowd had gathered to hear the famous preacher George Whitefield. Marrant planned to play a prank by loudly tooting his horn. Before he had a chance, however, he heard the preacher's words and took them to heart.

Now a bold young man of faith, Marrant carried his Bible and a book of hymns with him wherever he went. His family disapproved of his new religion, so he left Charleston and headed into the wilderness just outside the city. Sleeping high in a tree at night to escape being eaten by a pack of wolves, he ate grass to survive during the day, until he stumbled upon a Cherokee hunting in the woods. They traveled together for a couple of months. But when he entered a Cherokee village, Marrant was tied up and threatened to be killed—in spite of the protests of his new friend! However, when his captives heard Marrant praying and reading his Bible, they wanted to learn about his faith. So they untied

John Marrant (1755–c. 1791)

After the American Revolution, John Marrant became a Methodist minister. He traveled to Novia Scotia as a missionary, and then eventually moved to Boston. Ordained by Prince Hall (see page 108), Marrant became a Mason in African Lodge 459 where he was chaplain of the lodge. In 1789, he delivered a powerful antislavery sermon at the lodge to celebrate the Festival of St. John. Along with his autobiography, this sermon was also published.

Courtesy of Ashmolean Museum, University of Oxford

him and treated him as an honored guest. Armed braves then escorted him from village to village so he could share his religion among the various tribes.

Marrant eventually returned home. Because he was dressed like a Native American and carrying a tomahawk, his family didn't recognize him. He finally convinced them that he really was their long lost son and brother.

His life returned to normal, but not for long. War broke out between the colonists and the British—the American Revolution had begun. The British Navy kidnapped young Marrant and forced him to play as a musician on board ship for seven years. He was finally released in London after the war was over.

Alice (1686-1804)

A lice loved history because she lived it. She was eyewitness to over 100 years of our nation's founding history.

Her parents were some of the first people of African descent to arrive in Philadelphia, and were slaves from Barbados. Alice was born into slavery in 1686. At that time, Philadelphia was little more than a wilderness. Cougars screamed and wolves howled in the woods surrounding the wigwams, huts, and cabins of the settlement. Native Americans hunted wild game nearby and traded with the pioneers.

When Alice was 10 years old, her master moved his family and slaves from Philadelphia to nearby Dunk's Ferry. She was 15 when William Penn granted a charter to the city of Philadelphia before he traveled back to England. Alice remembered William Penn well. For over 40 years, she also collected fares from travelers at Dunk's Ferry, where she lived the rest of her long, long life.

Alice was in her 40s when Independence Hall was being built. She was in her 60s when people first heard the Liberty Bell, known at that time as the State House Bell. She was 90 when the Declaration of Independence was signed. And when President George Washington arrived in Philadelphia, the new nation's temporary capital, Alice was 104 years old.

Throughout her later years, Alice became famous locally as an oral historian. When she visited Philadelphia, many notable people called on her to ask her about the history of the city. She never tired of pointing out historic landmarks and describing events she'd seen with her very own eyes. Alice lived to be 116 years old.

Courtesy of the Library Company of Philadelphia

Slave Life in the North

Plantations and small farms in the North, as well as numerous industries in growing cities, needed a steady supply of workers. Indentured servants couldn't arrive fast enough from the European countries to meet this labor demand.

As slave ships began to sail farther and farther north along the coast of colonial America, more and more colonists purchased enslaved Africans. Ships arrived to offer a growing supply.

Historical records are vague about when the first Africans arrived in chains in the northern colonies. New Amsterdam, or New York as it is known today, probably introduced slavery soon after the colony was founded in 1624. The governor of the Massachusetts Bay Company, John Winthrop, wrote in his *Journal* that in 1638, Africans arrived in Boston along with other cargo on board the ship *Desire*. In 1684, 150 Africans arrived in Philadelphia on board the *Isabella*.

Enslaved Africans were put to work in a variety of jobs throughout the northern colonies. Many held domestic positions such as personal maids or caregivers. Women cooked in iron pots over hot flames. They toted water for washing clothes. As valets, men took responsibility for trimming and powdering the fashionable wigs worn by the colonists of that day. They cared for the horses and drove the carriages. They chopped down trees in the new settlements and constructed sturdy buildings.

African Americans were watchmakers, shoemakers, bookbinders, and cabinetmakers. They were blacksmiths, bricklayers, tanners, weavers, and sailmakers. They were bakers, barbers, and doctors. They worked in shipyards to build ships. They sailed the seven seas as sailors, whalers, and ships' crews. All throughout the North as well as the South, African Americans were influential in shaping the daily life and industry of colonial America.

Briton Hammon's Journey

One of the earliest documents to be published in America gives us a glimpse of what life was like for African Americans during colonial days. In his autobiography, Briton Hammon describes the amazing 13-year journey he took after signing up in Plymouth, Massachusetts, to ship on board a sloop, or sailing vessel, bound for Jamaica. The journey started out pleasantly enough and the crew reached Jamaica in about 30 days. After loading the hold with wood, the sloop headed north, and Hammon's dangerous adventures began.

The sloop struck a reef off the coast of Florida, and Hammon was captured by Native Americans. After being held for several weeks, he was taken to Havana and sold into service in the Spanish governor's castle. One day, he was kidnapped by a press-gang rounding up sailors to board the king of Spain's ships and sail to Spain. Hammon refused to set sail, so they tossed him in the dungeon, locked him up, and threw away the key. Hammon tried to send word to the governor about his misfortunes, but nobody would help him. Finally, four and a half years later, the governor discovered where he was.

Released immediately, Hammon was put back into service at the governor's castle. One of his new duties was to help carry a large red velvet chair around the region to transport the local bishop. After attempting several escapes, he secretly boarded an English ship that had stopped in port. The Spanish governor demanded his return to captivity, but the English captain refused. Hammon sailed safely to London and eventually back home to Boston.

The entrance of Havana, from within the harbor.
Courtesy of the Library of Congress, Prints & Photographs Division, LC-USZ62-46051

Briton Hammon

NARRATIVE
Of the
UNCOMMON SUFFERINGS,
AND
Surprizing DELIVERANCE
OF
Briton Hammon,
A Negro Man,---- Servant to
GENERAL WINSLOW,
Of *Marſhfield*, in NEW-ENGLAND;

Who returned to *Boſton*, after having
been abſent almoſt Thirteen Years.

CONTAINING

An Account of the many Hardſhips he underwent from
the Time he left his Maſter's Houſe, in the Year 1747,
to the Time of his Return to *Boſton*.—How he was
Caſt away in the Capes of *Florida* ;---the horrid Cru-
elty and inhuman Barbarity of the *Indians* in murder-
ing the whole Ship's Crew ;---the Manner of his being
carry'd by them into Captivity. Alſo, An Account of
his being Confined Four Years and Seven Months
in a cloſe Dungeon,---And the remarkable Manner in
which he met with his *good old Maſter* in *London* ; who
returned to *New-England*, a Paſſenger, in the ſame Ship.

BOSTON, Printed and Sold by GREEN & RUSSELL,
in Queen-Street. 1760.

Briton Hammon's *Narrative.*
Courtesy of the Library of Congress, Rare Books and Special Collections Division

Briton Hammon lived the dangerous life usually found only in the pages of a swashbuckling adventure book. In Boston in 1760, he published the 14-page account of his hair-raising adventures as *A Narrative of the Uncommon Sufferings, and Surprizing Deliverance of Briton Hammon, A Negro Man*. It is often regarded as the first autobiography or slave narrative published by an African American.

The Princes

From the day Africans first arrived in chains in the English colonies, various individuals as well as entire groups of those who were enslaved sought freedom and fought to be free. Abijah Prince, a former slave, is thought to have earned his freedom because of his service in the French and Indian War. He also purchased the freedom of his wife, Lucy Terry Prince.

Born in Africa, kidnapped as an infant, and brought to America on a slave ship, Lucy Terry grew up enslaved to a master in Deerfield, Massachusetts. She is best known as the first African American poet in America.

When Lucy Terry was 16 years old, she witnessed an attack on colonists by Native Americans near her home at a place called The Bars. Her poem, "Bar's Fight" describes the massacre. Her poem was read each year at community events and was published 100 years later in the book, *History of Western Massachusetts*.

Together, Abijah and Lucy Terry Prince raised six children. Following in the footsteps of their father and demonstrating the courageous spirit of their mother, two of their sons fought in the American Revolution.

Lucy Terry Prince (c. 1730–1821)

Nobody made trouble for Lucy Terry Prince and got away with it. When wealthy white neighbors tore down her fences and set her haystacks on fire, Prince fought back—and won! She took her protest to the governor's council, and they voted in her favor. When another neighbor decided to draw up his own property lines—including some of her land—Prince took the case all the way to Vermont's Supreme Court. She hired a leading lawyer of the day but then changed her mind and decided to defend herself. Good thing she did—after stating her argument and explaining that this land had been granted to her husband by King George III himself, the presiding judge said Prince argued "better than he had heard from any lawyer at the Vermont Bar." She won the case and kept her family's land.

"It Becomes Necessary for One People to Dissolve the Political Bands . . ."

★ ★ ★

YEARS OF UNREST

In his own little world, growing up in his teens and working as a slave on a small plantation near Dover, Delaware, Richard Allen struggled with the issues of freedom and liberty. Each morning when he heard the rooster crow and opened his eyes from slumber, he knew the day ahead of him would be filled with hard work—the work of a slave.

Being "owned" by a master worried Allen constantly. His master, Stokeley Sturgis, did not manage his finances well. He was very much in debt, and eventually sold Allen's mother and three younger siblings to pay off some debts. Allen's older sister and brother remained behind with him.

The uncertainty of his own future weighed constantly on his mind. Would the aging Sturgis die suddenly and Allen be sold to pay off his debts? Would he forever be a slave, always living under the shadow of another person's authority and demands?

Field of grain near Dover, Delaware, in the vicinity where Richard Allen tended crops while enslaved on the plantation owned by Stokeley Sturgis.
Courtesy of Mike Mahaffie, mahaffie.blogspot.com

During this time of Allen's personal struggles, the American colonies were struggling as well. Colonists protested most of the new laws that King George III pronounced, laws that restricted basic freedoms and liberties. The Quartering Act forced colonists to allow British troops to live in their homes. The Sugar Act restricted supplies to America from any other country except England. The Stamp Act forced colonists to pay for a stamp to put on their documents. Many American colonists, both black and white, felt as if the king were trying to make them his slaves.

All throughout the 13 colonies, the colonists expressed their distaste and disregard for the king's new laws.

The Boston Massacre

On March 5, 1770, a crowd gathered at the wharfs in Boston. Tensions were high. Colonists were resentful of the British troops stationed in their city. They were angry about the new taxes and new laws King George III was forcing upon them.

A tall figure gathered the crowd together. Standing six feet two inches, Crispus Attucks was known as a leader among his fellow whalers, sailors, and dockworkers. He led the colonists away from Dock Square and through the streets of Boston.

Attucks and the other colonists marched toward King Street. Bells rang out, alerting the citizens that trouble was in the air. By now, a small group of British soldiers stood in front of the Customs House with bayonets and muskets.

By the time Attucks and his group arrived, there were 300 to 400 people gathered in the angry crowd. Colonists pelted the British soldiers with snowballs, bits of sharp ice, and stones. The British soldiers fired. Attucks fell to the ground dead. Four other men were also killed, and several more wounded. The soldiers who fired were arrested and put in prison to be tried for murder.

For the next couple of days, mourners honored the heroism of Crispus Attucks and one of the other men as their bodies lay in state at Faneuil Hall. The day of the funeral, stores closed and church bells rang. Thousands followed along the funeral procession to the Old Granary Burial Ground where Attucks and the four other men were buried in one common grave.

March 5 became known as Crispus Attucks Day. Over the years, special celebrations were held, such as in Boston in 1858 when Crispus Attucks Day was celebrated with speeches and a display of historical artifacts. In 1888, at the repeated recommendation of both black and white abolitionists, the city of Boston unveiled the Crispus Attucks monument to honor this great American hero and the others who gave their lives that day.

On the Affray in King-Street, on the Evening of the 5th of March, 1770

BY PHILLIS WHEATLEY

With Fire enwrapped, surcharged with sudden Death,
Lo, the poised Tube convolves its fatal Breath!
The flying Ball with heaven-directed Force,
Rids the free Spirit of its fallen Corse*

Well fated shades! Let no unmanly Tear
From Pity's Eye, distain your honored Bier*:
Lost to their View, surviving Friends may mourn,
Yet over thy pile shall Flames celestial burn;

Long as in *Freedom's* Cause the Wise contend,
Dear to your country shall your Fame extend;
While to the World, the lettered *Stone* shall tell,
How *Caldwell, Attucks, Gray* and *Maverick* fell.

*A corse is a corpse, or body of someone who died.

*A bier is something used to carry a corpse or coffin to the cemetery or burial ground.

This poem appeared unsigned and without title in the March 12, 1770, issue of the *Boston Evening Post*. It is attributed to Phillis Wheatley.

Courtesy of the Library of Congress

Make a Stamp

The Stamp Act of 1765 placed an official tax on paper documents. Any petition, bill, newspaper, inventory, certificate, or document written on paper was taxed under the new law. Even playing cards!

The Stamp Act affected everyone. If a group of free blacks wanted to write a petition against slavery and send it to the courts, they would have to pay a tax on the document. If a man who was enslaved bought his freedom and was given manumission papers declaring he would be forever free, a tax would have to be paid.

Adult supervision required

Materials

- ★ Paper
- ★ Pencil
- ★ Scissors
- ★ Craft foam
- ★ Glue
- ★ Toothpicks
- ★ 2- to 3-inch plastic lid from a bottle, such as laundry detergent
- ★ Black craft paint or stamp pad

1. Draw your stamp design on a sheet of paper. Be sure this design will fit on the flat end of the lid.

2. Once done, cut out the design using scissors, flip it over, and trace it onto a piece of craft foam.

3. Use scissors to cut out the stamp design from the craft foam.

4. Use a toothpick to spread glue on the craft foam, then glue it to the flat part of the lid.

5. When the glue is dry, press the stamp into a small puddle of paint or onto a stamp pad.

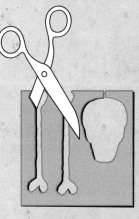

6. Practice your stamp several times on scrap paper before putting your "official" stamp on the paper or letter you choose.

Draw a Political Cartoon

Numerous political cartoons appeared that expressed the angry feelings of the colonists against decisions enforced by King George III, such as the Stamp Act. Most of these cartoons, though not necessarily all of them, were one single picture. Many were published in leading newspapers of the day.

Materials

★ Drawing paper

★ Pencils

★ Pens

Think of a topic that is important to you. It can be a controversial topic that two sides argue about, such as the Stamp Act. It can be an important event in history. It can be about an upcoming holiday. Your political cartoon can be about something currently in the news—either in your local school or community, your state, the nation, or the world.

Start with a pencil and drawing paper. Sketch various basic ideas for your political cartoon. Some political cartoons show an important person drawn as an animal. Other political cartoons, such as the one of the people of Boston tarring and feathering the tax man, show a picture of what people are thinking of doing about a certain situation, even if they wouldn't really do it.

Draw a simple pencil sketch of your cartoon. When you are finished, make sure that it conveys the message you want to say. Some political cartoons give characters speech balloons with clever sayings. Choose a caption or title for the cartoon that sums up its meaning in one simple word or phrase.

Use a pen to finish drawing the cartoon. You can draw right on top of the pencil sketch and then erase the pencil lines. Or, simply use your pencil sketch as a reference. When you are done, write your signature or your initials at the bottom of the picture. Photocopy your cartoon. After sharing it with your parent or teacher, place the photocopy flat in a large envelope and mail it to your school newsletter or community newspaper. Perhaps it will get published.

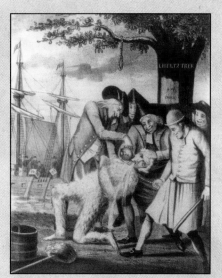

Political cartoon of tarring and feathering the tax man in Boston.

Courtesy of the Library of Congress, Prints and Photographs Division, LC-USZ62-1308

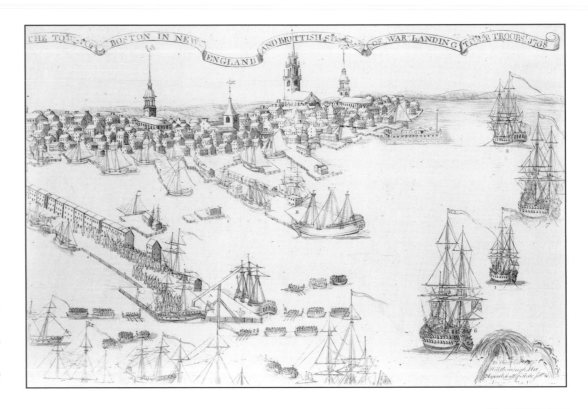

(clockwise from the right)

British warships landing their troops at Boston.
*Courtesy of the Library of Congress, Prints &
Photographs Division, LC-USZ62-134241*

Crispus Attucks at the Boston Massacre.
*Used with Permission of Documenting the American South,
the University of North Carolina at Chapel Hill Libraries*

Faneuil Hall, Boston, where the body of Crispus Attucks
and another hero of the Boston Massacre lay in state.
Courtesy National Archives (208-PR-10D-1)

Boston: A Seedbed of Freedom

Crispus Attucks showed the world that African Americans were among the names of influential colonists daring to hope for freedom. As tensions grew, more and more African Americans stepped forward to mark their footprints on the pages of American history. Many of these Black Founders joined the ranks of patriotic colonists within the city of Boston, that hotbed of protest that seethed with turmoil and became known as the seedbed of freedom.

Just one month after the Boston Massacre, a paper was written up and handed to a slave in Boston. No angry protests for freedom accompanied this simple act. But for Prince Hall of Boston, a former slave now set free, the manumission paper changed his life. Forever.

Beginning with the community of free blacks in Boston and extending his reach throughout the newly forming nation, Hall and the African American leaders who rose up around him, changed and shaped the course of American history in remarkable and astonishing ways.

Crispus Attucks (c. 1723–March 5, 1770)

His father was African. His mother was Native American. And Crispus Attucks was a full-blooded American hero. The flame of freedom burned in his heart, even though he was enslaved. When he was 27 years old, he dared to escape. Ads appeared in the *Boston Gazette* that offered 10 pounds for his capture. Once free, however, Attucks was determined to stay free. He sailed aboard whaling vessels, traveling in and out of New England ports.

Attucks felt the sting of oppression. In Boston on the evening of March 5, 1770, he led a group of angry sailors and dockworkers. Carrying stout clubs, they marched from Dock Square to King Street. Attucks led the cry for freedom from British tyranny. Shots rang out, and Attucks entered the halls of history as the first to die in the cause for freedom during the era of the American Revolution.

Courtesy of the Library of Congress, Prints & Photographs Division, LC-USZ62-59669

Jupiter Hammon (1711–c. 1806)

As far as Jupiter Hammon was concerned, both blacks and whites, free and enslaved, were suffering in spiritual bondage. He wrote poetry, sermons, and essays to voice his passionate concern. On Christmas Day, 1769, he published *An Evening Thought: Salvation by Christ, with Penitential Cries.* It was the first poem published by an African American.

Hammon lived on Long Island, New York, in the home of rich merchants. Enslaved for his entire life, he worked for several generations of the family as a clerk and a bookkeeper.

He pursued a higher cause, however. He worked hard at extra jobs until he earned enough money to purchase his own Bible. He sprinkled the verses of his poetry with verses of Scripture. His poem, *An Address to Miss Phillis Wheatley,* praises her for her strong and devout faith. Probably his most famous and well-known publication was *An Address to the Negroes in the State of New York.* Written when he was over 70 years old, it was addressed to the members of New York City's African Society and was reprinted several times.

Scipio Moorhead

Creative spirit. Artistic talent. Sensitivity to detail. These were the characteristics of Scipio Moorhead, whom historians credit with painting the unsigned portrait of Phillis Wheatley that appeared in the front of her book. It was the first time a portrait of an African American was published, and it shows proof of the amazing talent and ability of the artist.

Beyond this portrait, and a poem Wheatley wrote in honor of a young black painter assumed to be Moorhead, history is silent except for one fact: Scipio Moorhead was enslaved and living in Boston at the same time as Phillis Wheatley.

Their paths crossed, verse was exchanged for picture, and together a young man and young woman who had descended from Africa's shores shaped the future of America.

A Poet Speaks

In the years leading up to the outbreak of war, British soldiers marched through the streets of Boston to the taunts of "Lobsterbacks" and "Redcoats." Colonists, both black and white, protested loudly and visibly against King George's taxes and attempts at taking control of their freedoms.

Right in the middle of all the unrest, an unexpected voice was heard. A poetess from Africa's shores who now lived, enslaved, on King Street in Boston, took pen in hand and rocked the world.

She was named after the slave ship, *Phillis*, that carried her to Boston. She was given the same last name as her new masters, John and Susanna Wheatley. Her front baby teeth were missing, so they guessed her age to be about seven years old. She was raised to be a household slave.

Young Phillis Wheatley, however, had a mind of her own. Eager for an education, she learned to read and write. She devoured classic poetry and studied Latin. By the time she was about 14, her own poems were being published in colonial newspapers.

John and Susanna Wheatley were members of a church affiliated with Loyalists. Unlike her masters, however, Phillis Wheatley decided to attend Old South Meeting House, a center for patriot activity and a meeting place for the Sons of Liberty.

A common theme ran through many of Wheatley's poems and expressed her cry for liberty. She carried the torch of freedom and wrote poetry expressing her patriotic passion. Her voice, enslaved as she was, rang out as a champion for freedom from British rule. Her writings gave a glimpse into what it was like to be descended from the shores of Africa, yet living in colonial America.

In her poetry, Wheatley often referred to herself as "Afric's muse." During this era, many people mistakenly saw Africa as a barbaric continent. Even famous "learned" men and women in colonial America simply did not understand the great culture and advanced learning that existed among the cities and nations of Africa. Most colonists knew nothing about Africa's glorious past during the Middle Ages when cities such as Timbuktu, Jenne, and Kano were great centers of academics, commerce, and culture.

The name of Phillis Wheatley became so well known in colonial Boston that she decided to publish a book in England featuring a collection of her poems. She suffered from breathing problems that appeared to be related to asthma. Always in frail health, doctors suggested that a trip to London might be good for her, especially to breathe the sea air. The Wheatleys' son was traveling to London at the time, so it was decided that Phillis would accompany him. Once there, she hoped to oversee the publication of her book.

It was during her stay in London that she met many influential people who came to honor the famous American poet from Africa. Benjamin Franklin, in England at the time, was among her list of noted visitors. Her trip was cut short, however, when an ailing Susanna Wheatley requested her return home.

Phillis Wheatley (Peters) (c. 1753-1784)

Phillis Wheatley grew up a slave in Boston in the midst of great political turmoil. She chose to side fervently with the patriots.

When the Boston Massacre took place, she honored Crispus Attucks and the heroes of the day by writing the poem, "On the Affray in King Street, on the Evening of the 5th of March, 1770." When King George III repealed the dreaded Stamp Act, she praised the decision and wrote the poem, "To The King's Most Excellent Majesty on his Repealing the American Stamp Act." George Washington arranged a private meeting with her after she wrote a poem in his honor. She rejoiced to commemorate the signing of the Paris Peace Treaty in her poem, "Liberty and Peace."

Phillis Wheatley was the first African American to publish a book. *Poems on Various Subjects, Religious and Moral* hit the printing presses in 1773. She was also a fiery patriot who hoped that the American Revolution would bring an end to slavery. Driven by these hopes and passionate beliefs, she determined to use her pen and influence her world for the cause of freedom.

Courtesy of Library of Congress, Rare Book and Special Collections, LC-USZ62-12533

Camp Meetings in the Forest

While trouble was brewing throughout the original colonies, Richard Allen experienced troubles of his own. At 17 years old, he felt lost and alone, overwhelmed with the burdens he already carried at his young age. The fears of his uncertain future weighed heavily on young Richard's heart. Around this time, a Methodist camp meeting was set up in the forest near his home. Preachers came to preach the Bible, and teachers came to teach it. Blacks and whites alike, both enslaved and free, were invited to come.

One evening, Allen visited the camp meeting. Many of his friends and fellow slaves from neighboring plantations were there. There was no separate seating; blacks and whites, slaves and masters, sat on benches together, stood in small circles, or knelt on the ground in prayer. All waited together, eager for the preacher to begin.

The sermon started. Hearing the preacher's words, troubled thoughts filled young Richard's mind. He listened to the preacher and wrestled with an important decision. Finally, he made his choice. He decided to accept the Christian faith.

> "I cried unto Him who delighteth to hear the prayers of a poor sinner; and all of a sudden my dungeon shook, my chains flew off."
>
> —Richard Allen

Suddenly, for the first time in his entire life, Allen tasted freedom. It was a glorious thing! His heart was as light as a feather. He visited his friends who worked at neighboring plantations and told them about his newfound faith. He talked with others who had been Christians for a long time. He was eager to learn more.

Allen joined the Methodist society. For several years, he attended the camp meetings held in the forest. His oldest brother and sister also accepted the same faith he now followed. Every week, they attended class meetings in the forest where a class leader taught them to read the Bible. Every other Thursday, a preacher arrived to preach to the listening crowd in Allen's neighborhood.

A Secret Plan

Local plantation owners and white neighbors complained to Stokeley Sturgis. They said that he shouldn't allow his slaves to attend the camp meetings. They said it would give them new ideas about freedom and self-worth and equal rights. When Richard found out what the neighbors were saying, he and his brother came up with a secret plan. They decided to work extra hard each day in the fields. Their plan was to show Stokeley Sturgis that religion would improve every person in every way, both black and white, slave and free. Their plan was to soften their master's heart so that he would be open to listening to the traveling Methodist preachers who taught

A camp meeting.
Courtesy of the Library of Congress, Prints & Photographs Division, LC-USZ62-63867

29

about freedom—freedom for people's souls and freedom for slaves. Deep in the hearts of Richard and his brother, they hoped that their master would one day join the Methodists, and set his slaves free.

It was some time after this that Richard Allen spoke privately with Stokeley Sturgis. Richard said he would like to ask the Methodist preachers to come preach at the house so Stokeley and his wife could hear. Stokeley asked his wife about it, and both agreed that they liked this idea.

The next Wednesday, the preacher came to the plantation where Allen lived. Every Wednesday after that for several months, preachers came and taught about the Bible. Many Methodist ministers, including those who now visited Allen's home, gave fiery sermons against slavery. Soon Stokeley Sturgis took the preachers' words to heart. He determined that slavery was against the principles of the Bible. One day, he proposed to Allen and his brother that they could buy their freedom.

Two Thousand Continental Dollars

Stokeley Sturgis made a deal with Richard Allen and his brother. If they could pay him 2,000 Continental dollars or 60 pounds in gold and silver, they could be free.

The sweet liberty that he had dreamed of was now within his grasp—if only he could earn enough money fast enough to purchase it before his old master died. With a determination he would demonstrate for the rest of his life, he set his heart on earning the money. Though his hands were soon covered with blisters, he chopped as much wood as he could sell. He worked long hours in a brickyard making bricks. Whatever his hands could do, so stiff and sore that he could barely open or close them, Allen worked hard and furious and fast.

Finally, he bought his freedom. Set free— what a glorious day! Stokeley Sturgis signed the manumission papers, legal documents that declared his slave named Richard was forever free.

> "We often thought that after our master's death we were liable to be sold to the highest bidder, as he was much in debt; and thus my troubles were increased, and I was often brought to weep."
> —Richard Allen

> "I Do hereby . . . Manumit Exonerate Release and for Ever Discharge and set at final Liberty the said Negro Man named Richard."
> —from Richard Allen's manumission papers written by Stokeley Sturgis

Richard Allen experienced a personal rebirth in the same years and in the exact same place as a new nation was being birthed. And while the history of this new nation was being made, Allen stepped into freedom and began to make his mark on the history of the nation. Soon, he would establish his place as one of the Black Founders of America.

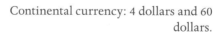

Continental currency: 4 dollars and 60 dollars.
Courtesy of Mac's Old Paper Money: Colonial & Continental Currency

"We Hold These Truths to Be Self-Evident . . ."

★ ★ ★

BEGINNINGS OF WAR

What an amazing thing it was for young Richard Allen to rise up out of the oppression of slavery, take his future into his own hands, and break off the chains of an established institution. Link by link, chain by chain, he broke the unbreakable. He planned the unthinkable. He focused his entire being on one goal: freedom.

Deep in his heart, Allen felt that it was his right to pursue his own freedom. He had spent his early years in Benjamin Chew's household where he overheard many conversations about the rights people had. He had attended camp meetings where Methodist preachers preached against the evils of slavery and explained the value of each individual's soul. Talk was everywhere about liberty and freedom from English rule. In circles both large and small, everyone was discussing the "Rights of Man," freedoms and rights every single person should have.

Crispus Attucks in the Boston Massacre, March 5, 1770.
Courtesy National Archives (69-N-4877-C)

Petitions from Boston

In Boston, African Americans caught the fire of freedom. In the years 1773 and 1774, five petitions from enslaved African Americans in Boston were submitted to the General Court of Massachusetts assembled in Boston. Each petition made its mark in history and stands forever as a powerful symbol of human dignity. The cry for freedom rings out across the centuries through the words of these petitions to reveal a hunger for human rights and equality.

The first petition was "the humble petition of many slaves, living in the town of Boston, and other towns in the province." Submitted on January 6, 1773, the unidentified voices cried out, "We have no property. We have no wives. No children. We have no city. No country. But we have a Father in Heaven. . . ." The petitioners committed themselves to bearing the responsibilities of colonial life, if only they would be given their freedom and thus be allowed to do so. The petition is signed simply, "Felix." It was soon published in pamphlet form for everyone to read.

The second petition was submitted from Boston on April 20, 1773. Its opening paragraph boldly declared, "The efforts made by the legislative of this province in their last sessions to free themselves from slavery, gave us, who are in that deplorable state, a high degree of satisfaction. We expect great things from men who have made such a noble stand against the designs of their fellow-men to enslave them." In this petition, Boston's African American community asked for one day a week to work for their own pay so they could raise money to travel back to Africa and build a settlement. It was signed by four leaders on behalf of their fellow slaves: Peter Bestes, Sambo Freeman, Felix Holbrook, and Chester Joie.

Shortly after this petition, a third was submitted to the General Court of Massachusetts in June of 1773. Only a portion of it remains, but the heartfelt cry rings out, "Your petitioners apprehend they have in common with other men a natural right to be free."

The fourth petition was submitted a year later on May 25, 1774. This one describes how the petitioners had been stolen from their homelands and brought to this country only to be made slaves. Here, they were denied the privilege of marriage, their children were sold far away from them, and they lived in deplorable conditions. "We therefore beg your Excellency and Honors will give this its due weight and consideration and that you will accordingly cause an act of the legislative to be passed that we may obtain our natural right, our freedoms, and our children be set at liberty at the year of twenty-one."

A similar, revised petition was again submitted in June 1774. This petition, the fifth one from Boston, was submitted on "behalf

Petition signed in 1773 by Peter Bestes, Sambo Freeman, Felix Holbrook, and Chester Joie.

Collection of the New York Historical Society, Negative #51012

of all those, who, by divine permission, are held in a state of slavery, within the bowels of a free country." The petitioners asked "that all of us . . . may be liberated and made free men of this community, and be entitled to all privileges and immunities of its free and natural born subjects."

Even though the response from the General Court of Massachusetts was the same for all five petitions and none of them were granted, these early efforts were not in vain. Together, they were like an earthquake that rocked the world. These petitions set in motion a tidal wave that gathered strength and crashed over the land. They set the stage for future petitions of freedom. They influenced countless abolitionists, both black and white, to work together to bring an end to slavery in Massachusetts as well as end the trans-Atlantic slave trade. These beginning efforts reached far forward across the years to influence amazing leaders such as Frederick Douglass to bring an end to slavery in the Civil War, to inspire back-to-Africa movements led by such greats as Martin R. Delany and Marcus Garvey, and to compel civil rights heroes such as Dr. Martin Luther King Jr. to lead the march toward equal rights.

Peter Bestes, Sambo Freeman, Felix Holbrook, Chester Joie

We know nothing about the personal lives of these men, but we know they were leaders of the enslaved African American community in Boston. On April 20, 1773, they put their names on a petition requesting, among other things, the right for slaves to work one day a week for themselves in order to raise enough money to move back to Africa.

Just as the men who signed the Declaration of Independence knew their signatures could mean their death sentence, these four men were willing to put their lives at stake in the interest of all the other slaves throughout the province. These four Black Founders ran the risk of the anger of colonists who did not wish to give slaves any rights or freedoms. They were willing to give up their lives for the freedom of others.

Joining In the Fight

Boston wasn't the only place where the fire of liberty burned bright and strong. The First Continental Congress met in the fall of 1774. Soon word was sent throughout every colony to form military protection. African Americans throughout the North and the South responded to the call. Free blacks as well as slaves signed their names to muster rolls for local militias. These men drilled side by side with their friends and neighbors, both black and white.

In New York City in 1775, some historians say that slaves pulled down the statue of King George III. In Charleston in 1776, there were reports that enslaved African Americans marched through the streets protesting for their rights and freedom. All throughout the colonies, African Americans joined the cause for liberty and human rights.

Artist's interpretation of the historic day when the statue of King George III was pulled down in New York City.
Courtesy of the Library of Congress, Prints & Photographs Division, LC-USZ62-22023

Black Masons

On March 5, 1775, a crowd gathered at Phillis Wheatley's church, the Old South Meeting Hall in Boston. A memorial was being held to honor the fifth anniversary of the Boston Massacre, the night when Crispus Attucks and four other patriots gave their lives. Tensions ran high that night. British troops arrived at the meeting to make sure the colonists didn't say anything against King George III. After the ceremony, rumors of a fire nearly incited a riot, and a short skirmish broke out between the colonists and the British soldiers.

The very next night, on March 6, 1775, Prince Hall and a group of free blacks from Boston walked quickly through the dark streets. Step by step, they were on their way to make a monumental mark on history.

At that time, there were no organized groups for African Americans to join. Prince Hall, however, was about to change all that. He was determined to join the society of Masons.

Hall's goal was total freedom for all blacks. His vision included an end to slavery in the colony of Massachusetts where he lived, as well as an end to the trans-Atlantic slave trade. He dreamed of bringing an end to the institution of slavery itself. He knew it would be a long, uphill struggle, but he was willing to dedicate his life. Forming a society of black Masons was the first step toward reaching his goal.

Hall first tried to join with colonial Masonic lodges in the Boston area. Each time he applied for membership, however, he was turned away. Finally, he decided to apply for membership with the British Masons. There was a lodge of British Masons among the troops stationed in Boston who accepted his request.

Hall and the other free blacks found their way to this British lodge. They were invited inside and formally initiated that night into the secret rites of Freemasonry.

Less than two weeks later, Hall received a permit allowing him to organize a separate lodge for African Americans. This gave him the freedom to meet with his new fellow Masons on their own.

It was a good thing Hall took the steps to form his own separate lodge from the British. Relationships between Britain and the American colonists were getting worse. Trouble was brewing. Everyone was preparing for war.

The Shot Heard Round the World

Local militias had been organized to protect towns throughout the colonies. When the call to arms had first spread throughout the countryside, many brave men, both black and white, signed up to serve as Minutemen.

In Lexington, Massachusetts, Prince Estabrook joined the ranks of Minutemen.

Everyone was talking about freedoms, rights, and liberties. These were powerful words that held deep meaning for the American colonists during the founding years of our country. How much more meaning did these words have for African Americans, when they dared to fight in defense of liberties they were often denied?

Yet dare to fight they did. With hope for freedom, Prince Estabrook enlisted as a Lexington Minuteman. Early on the morning of April 19, 1775, he heard the bells of Lexington ring, the beating of the drums, the gunshots, and the cries of alarm. Jerked out of sleep, he jumped out of bed, grabbed his musket, and ran through the dark to join the ranks of Minutemen gathered on Lexington Green. He waited in the chilly air. News was that British soldiers were marching out of Boston and heading toward Concord to destroy stockpiles of weapons and ammunition. The Redcoats reached Lexington first, however. Prince Estabrook and the Lexington Minutemen faced them bravely. The "shot heard round the world" rang out, others quickly followed, and the American Revolution began.

Memorial honoring Prince Estabrook.
Used with Permission of Charles H. Price Jr., Past Company Commander, Lexington Minute Men

Prince Estabrook (or Easterbrooks)

(c. 1740–1830)

Patriot. Minuteman. Founding Father. Prince Estabrook shouldered his musket and drilled with the Lexington Minutemen just outside of Boston on Lexington Green. When Paul Revere rode through the countryside crying, "The regulars are out!" Estabrook heard the alarm, grabbed his gun, and raced to Lexington Green. He stood brave and firm with the other Minutemen in the early hours before dawn on April 19, 1775, when British troops marched into view. Shots rang out, and Estabrook was listed among the wounded.

Known as the first African American to fight in the American Revolution, Estabrook was there at the very first battle of the war. After his wounds healed, he returned to fight. Records indicate that he served for the remainder of the war, including at Fort Ticonderoga in July 1776. At the end of the war, he was given his freedom.

In April 2008, a memorial was dedicated in front of Buckman Tavern to honor this brave hero of the American Revolution. Minute Man Charles Price, who for many years has portrayed Prince Estabrook in the yearly reenactment of the Battle of Lexington, spoke at the dedication.

Charles H. Price, Jr., Past Company Commander of the Lexington Minute Men, portrays Prince Estabrook.

Used with Permission of Charles H. Price, Jr., Past Company Commander, Lexington Minute Men

On to Concord

The entire countryside was alerted—British troops were heading to Concord! The citizens of Concord were busy that night and on into the early morning of April 19, 1775. They worked hard to hide as many supplies as they could. By dawn the Redcoats had arrived, following their previous skirmish with the Minutemen at Lexington.

Peter Salem marched with his unit throughout the town of Concord. He steadied his musket in his arms. He was known as an excellent shot, but could he stand up against His Majesty's royal troops? He glanced at the faces of the men marching among the ranks. Some were of African descent, like he was. They, too, were willing to risk their lives fighting for the precious hope of freedom—both from British rule and from slavery.

The Road Back to Boston

Fighting broke out at the North Bridge in Concord. After an unsuccessful campaign to destroy colonial military supplies, British troops began a dangerous retreat back to Boston. Many of their officers had been killed. Breaking ranks, the Redcoats turned and ran back to Boston and the safety of the British warships floating in the harbor.

All day long, colonial militias kept pouring in. Bells rang, calling the Minutemen to arms.

Historical accounts show that African Americans responded to the call, including David Lamson.

As British soldiers retreated, a group of 12 "exempts," men too old for military service, rallied to join the patriots. Today, these brave heroes are remembered as the "old men of Menotomy." Accounts differ of what took place that day, but some say that this group chose David Lamson as their leader.

Lamson was a natural leader, having fought in the French and Indian War. He knew the British would be coming down the road, so the 12 men gathered and crouched behind a low wall along the road to wait. Sure enough, British troops soon came into view. It was a convoy carrying wagonloads of supplies.

Lamson stood up with his companions and faced the British Army. When ordered to stop, however, the British ignored the colonials and whipped their horses to gallop faster along the road. Lamson and the 12 fired their muskets. Several Redcoats were killed or wounded. The others ran off across the countryside and later surrendered as prisoners. The supply wagons were captured.

David Lamson continued to serve in other terms of duty during the American Revolution. Today he is honored with a street named David Lamson Way in Arlington, Massachusetts.

Peter Salem (c. 1750–1816)

Peter Salem was born into slavery in Framingham, Massachusetts, not far from Lexington and Concord. Promised his freedom for enlisting, Salem was among the troops in Concord on the very first day of the war.

Known as an expert marksman, Salem is credited with shooting Major Pitcairn at the Battle of Bunker Hill. He later enlisted in the Continental Army when African Americans were permitted to join the ranks.

A dedicated and exemplary soldier, Salem suffered with the troops through the long, freezing winter of Valley Forge. He fought at major battles such as Saratoga and Stony Point. He served faithfully and bravely until the end of the war.

As a free citizen of the new nation, Salem returned to Massachusetts, married, and established a small farm. A skilled craftsman, he also was a weaver of cane and made baskets and chairs for a living. A tombstone at the gravesite of this Revolutionary War hero can be visited today.

Used with Permission of Documenting the American South, the University of North Carolina at Chapel Hill Libraries

The Black Paul Revere

In the community of Newmarket, New Hampshire, the town citizens elected a man named Wentworth Cheswill to be their town messenger for the Committee of Safety. Known today as the "Black Paul Revere," Cheswill rode throughout the town alerting patriots to urgent and important news.

It was no surprise that Wentworth Cheswill was elected to this important position. His family members were already known in the area as staunch patriots and pioneers. Around 1716, his grandfather Richard Cheswill, after being set free from slavery, bought land in the local area. The surviving deed is the oldest existing document showing proof of land owned by African Americans in New Hampshire. Wentworth's father, Hopestill Cheswill, also owned land and was a skillful carpenter who helped build such famous and historic buildings as the John Paul Jones House. Hopestill Cheswill was active in various aspects of community life as well.

After the American Revolution, Wentworth Cheswill continued to serve his hometown and community. He was elected to or volunteered in various town government positions including assessor, selectman, auditor, town clerk, school board member, and coroner. His love for history established him as the unofficial town historian. He became known for the historical artifacts and documents he collected about Newmarket, as well as notes he took of current events.

Wentworth Cheswill married at a young age. Together, he and his wife, Mary, had 13 children. His beautiful mansion was home to an extensive library of books, which he generously allowed others to borrow.

The Siege of Boston

By nightfall, after the battles of Lexington and Concord, British soldiers who hadn't been wounded, killed, or taken prisoner made it back to the safety of Boston. British warships floated in the harbor, offering them protection from further attack.

Meanwhile, the Minutemen followed the soldiers as closely as they dared. Camps were set up out of firing range from the cannons on the British warships, and the patriots settled in. They formed a type of blockade just outside of Boston, forcing the Redcoats to stay in the city. The Siege of Boston had begun.

In the weeks that followed, colonial troops and militias poured in from neighboring communities. Many African Americans, who had already been drilling with the troops to protect their own hometowns, now marched with their companies to the area surrounding Boston.

A Ballad of Freedom

Lemuel Haynes arrived to take part in the Siege of Boston, along with his militia from Granville, Massachusetts. Their encampment was at Roxbury, just outside of Boston.

Moved deeply by recent events, Haynes put pen to paper and wrote a stirring ballad. In the introduction to his historic poem "The Battle of Lexington," Haynes describes it as a "Poem on the inhuman Tragedy perpetrated on the 19th of April 1775 by a Number of the British Troops under the Command of Thomas Gage, which Parricides and Ravages are shocking Displays of ministerial & tyrannic Vengeance composed by Lemuel a young Mollato who obtained what little knowledge he possesses, by his own Application to Letters."

Wentworth Cheswill (or Cheswell) (1746–1817)

Wentworth Cheswill was a Black Founder in every way. Both his father and grandfather were important members of the community in Newmarket, New Hampshire, where they lived. Wentworth Cheswill was a vital part of colonial affairs. During the Revolutionary Era, he was elected town messenger for the Committee of Safety. Known today as the "Black Paul Revere," it was Cheswill's duty to ride throughout the neighboring community crying out the news. He also enlisted in the military and marched with his unit as part of the Saratoga campaign. After the end of the war, Cheswill was elected to numerous posts and governing positions in Newmarket. He helped shape the history of his hometown, as well as the history of the nation.

Signature of Wentworth Cheswill on his will.

Courtesy of Rockingham County Old Series Probate Record No. 9508, New Hampshire State Archives

The Battle of Lexington

By Lemuel Haynes

(SELECTED STANZAS)

———

The Nineteenth Day of April last
We ever shall retain
As monumental of the past
Most bloody shocking Scene

Then Tyrants filled with horrid Rage
A fatal Journey went
& Unmolested to engage
And slay the innocent

At Lexington they did appear
Arrayed in hostile Form
And tho our Friends were peaceful there
Yet on them fell the Storm

Eight most unhappy Victims fell
Into the Arms of Death
Unpitied by those Tribes of Hell
Who cursed them with their Breath

The Savage Band still march along
For Concord they were bound
While Oaths & Curses from their Tongue
Accent with hellish Sound

To prosecute their fell Desire
At Concord they unite
Two Sons of Freedom there expire
By their tyrannic Spite

Thus did our Friends endure their Rage
Without a murmuring Word
Till die they must or else engage
And join with one Accord

For Liberty, each Freeman Strives
As it's a Gift of God
And for it willing yield their Lives
And Seal it with their Blood

Thrice happy they who thus resign
Into the peaceful Grave
Much better there, in Death Confined
Than a Surviving Slave

This Motto may adorn their Tombs,
(Let tyrants come and view)
"We rather seek these silent Rooms
Than live as Slaves to You."

From the article "'The Battle of Lexington': A Patriotic Ballad by Lemuel Haynes" by Ruth Bogin in The William and Mary Quarterly, *3rd Ser., Vol. 42, No. 4 (Oct. 1985), 499–506.*

Pen a Patriotic Poem

To honor a great moment in history during colonial times, people often wrote a poem. Lemuel Haynes wrote "The Battle of Lexington." Phillis Wheatley wrote a poem about the Boston Massacre.

Now it's your turn! Write a patriotic poem about a great figure of African American history such as why Wentworth Cheswill is known as the "Black Paul Revere." Your poem could be about how he rode by horseback through the countryside, crying out the news.

There are many different kinds of poems you can write, such as a sonnet, a limerick, the haiku, a couplet, a triplet, a ballad, or an epic poem. Each of these kinds of poems follows very strict rules. Look up the rules before you try to write one yourself.

Original handwritten copy of Lemuel Haynes's ballad, "The Battle of Lexington."

By permission of the Houghton Library, Harvard University, bMS Am 1907(601)

Lemuel Haynes (1753-1833)

Lemuel Haynes knew the precious price men and women, both black and white, were willing to pay to experience a life of freedom. His father was from Africa, but he never knew him. His mother, a white colonist, refused to acknowledge him, and as an infant, he was indentured in the home of a white family in Granville, Massachusetts.

Having just finished his term of indenture, Haynes signed up as a Minuteman. He joined the Siege of Boston, and also served later on a campaign to march on Fort Ticonderoga.

Raised in a deeply religious home, Haynes embraced his faith as the true purpose of his life. After the war, he pursued the career of a minister. He studied under local pastors, after having taught himself by candlelight to further his limited schooling. He married, and he and his wife had 10 children.

Haynes became well-known and respected during the founding years of our country as a learned man of letters and powerful preacher and pastor of large congregations. He spoke frequently and wrote poems, sermons, and papers on a variety of topics, many of which can still be read today.

Used with Permission of Documenting the American South, the University of North Carolina at Chapel Hill Libraries

Surrounding the City of Boston

A number of African Americans marched with their troops to join the Siege of Boston. Salem Poor joined the siege with his company. Barzillai Lew arrived with his regiment, the Twenty-Seventh Massachusetts.

Barzillai Lew had also fought during the French and Indian War and was an experienced soldier. Records list Lew as a tall man, towering over others at six feet tall. He was about 30 years old during the Siege of Boston, and was listed as a cooper—a barrel maker—by trade. Known for his musical abilities, Lew was also a fifer and a drummer.

For nearly two months the men camped near Boston. Soldiers drilled as they waited for orders. Finally, the orders came. On June 16, 1775, patriot troops were sent secretly to Breed's Hill, overlooking the city of Boston. All night long, colonial soldiers dug with their shovels and picks to build dirt forts. When dawn broke the next morning of June 17, 1775, British troops and the entire city of Boston awoke and discovered to their shock that the patriots had taken command of the area we remember today as Bunker Hill.

The Battle of Bunker Hill

When the sun rose, British warships floating in the harbor immediately opened fire upon the colonial fortifications. Cannons roared as British troops organized on the docks of Boston's harbor, across the water and directly opposite the fortifications on Breed's Hill. Redcoats set the nearby town of Charlestown ablaze, which had earlier been evacuated during the siege.

The patriots, both black and white, waited safely behind the sturdy dirt walls they had built. Other colonial troops, out of reach of the cannons' deadly fire, were organized to build more fortifications. Finally, the British made their move. Troops were ferried across the river to where the patriots stood waiting. Once, twice, they marched forward and advanced toward the patriot lines. Both times the Redcoats were shot down. The third time they advanced, however, the patriots ran out of ammunition. British troops stormed over the walls, and the patriots retreated. Even though the British won the day, they suffered much heavier losses than the patriots. Many of their officers had been killed. The event became known as the Battle of Bunker Hill.

"The Flutist." Once thought to be Barzillai Lew, historians now credit this portrait as an unknown musician from the era following the American Revolution.
Courtesy of the Diplomatic Reception Rooms, U.S. Department of State, Washington, DC

African American patriots such as Barzillai Lew, Peter Salem, and Salem Poor fought at the Battle of Bunker Hill.
Courtesy National Archives (148-GW-448)

Write a New Verse for "Yankee Doodle"

Yankee Doodle went to town,
Riding on a pony.
Stuck a feather in his hat
And called it macaroni.

Chorus:
Yankee Doodle keep it up,
Yankee Doodle dandy.
Mind the music and the step,
And with the girls be handy.

When British troops were stationed in Boston, they felt they were superior to the ragtag Minutemen. Redcoats wore bright red uniforms, marched in orderly files, and were part of the most powerful army in the world. Minutemen, however, often dressed in homespun, homemade clothes, or buckskin. They were known for hiding behind rocks and shooting from behind trees, like Native Americans did, instead of always standing in organized lines like the British soldiers. There wasn't even an actual colonial army at first, just volunteers who would come and go, joining or leaving the fighting whenever they wanted to.

The British soldiers started singing "Yankee Doodle" while stationed in Boston to make fun of the Minutemen. When they marched into Lexington in the early dawn of April 19, 1775, some accounts note that their fifers played "Yankee Doodle."

Much to the surprise of the Redcoats, however, they met brave, organized fighting men both at Lexington and Concord. These patriots, instead of feeling ashamed, were proud of their ability to stand up and fight against the British. The patriots began to sing "Yankee Doodle" with gusto, and it became an immediate hit.

You can write a new verse to sing for "Yankee Doodle." Choose words that describe the pride you feel about being an American and living in the land of opportunity, freedom, and equality.

Heroes of the Day

The Battle of Bunker Hill, known to colonists as the Battle of Charlestown, was the first major battle of the American Revolution. During this historic day, Barzillai Lew was credited with playing "Yankee Doodle" to encourage the troops. Peter Salem is credited for shooting Major Pitcairn. And Salem Poor, of Colonel Frye's regiment, was cited as the hero of the day.

Not much information is known about the details of Salem Poor's activities that previous night and during the Battle of Bunker Hill. Among other things, he was credited with having shot British Lieutenant Colonel Abercrombie. After this historic day, however, 14 American officers wrote and signed a petition recommending Salem Poor for his heroic actions. The petition stated, "Salem Poor, of Col. Frye's regiment, Capt. Ames company, in the late Battle at Charlestown, behaved like an Experienced officer, as well as an Excellent Soldier." Not only was Salem Poor the brave hero of the very first major battle in the American Revolution, he went on to serve with the Continental Army.

Barzillai Lew (1743–1822)

Barzillai Lew's nickname, "Zeal," was a fitting title for this zealous Black Founder. A well-accomplished and professional musician, he carried his fife to the battlefield to inspire the troops to fight for freedom. He is credited with playing "Yankee Doodle" during the Battle of Bunker Hill.

Barzillai Lew is one of a long line of patriots in a large family of acclaimed musicians, abolitionists, and freedom fighters. His father, Primus, as well as he himself, fought in the French and Indian War. Born free, Barzillai Lew cherished freedom and enlisted for several terms of duty during the American Revolution. His grandson and great-grandsons served during the Civil War. According to family historians and military records, Lew and his descendants served in every major American war on up to modern day.

Salem Poor (c. 1742–1780)

Salem Poor is remembered as the hero of the Battle of Bunker Hill. After the battle, 14 officers wrote a petition requesting honor be paid to this exemplary soldier. No other soldier from this battle was honored in this way.

Poor continued to serve in the Continental Army and enlisted for a three-year term. He was at Valley Forge as well as other important campaigns throughout the war.

Two centuries later, during our bicentennial celebration, America paid honor to this Black Founder. The U.S. Postal Service dedicated a stamp to his memory.

The Petition

The subscribers begg leave, to Report to your Honorable House (which wee do in justice to the caracter of so Brave a Man), that, under Our Own observation, Wee declare that a Negro Man, called Salem Poor, of Col. Frye's regiment, Capt. Ames company, in the late Battle at Charlestown, behaved like an Experienced officer, as well as an Excellent Soldier, to set forth Particulars of his conduct would be tedious. Wee would Only begg leave to say in the Person of this said Negro Centers a brave and gallant soldier. The Reward due to so great and Distinguisht a Caracter, Wee submit to the Congress.

Cambridge, Dec. 1775

The Subscribers begg leave, to Report to your
Honble House, (which Wee do in justice to the
Caracter of so Brave a Man) that under
Our Own, observation, Wee declare that
A Negro Man, Called Salem Poor, of Col.
Fryes Regiment, Capt. Ames Company —
in the late Battle at Charlestown, behaved
like an Experienced officer, as Well as an
Excellent Soldier, to Set forth Particulars of the
Conduct Would be Tedious, Wee Would Only
begg leave to Say in the Person of this Sd
Negro Centers a Brave & gallant Soldier
The Reward due to so great and Distinguisht a
Caracter, Wee Submit to the Congress —

Cambridge Decbr 5th 1775   Jonas Brewer Col
                            Thomas Nixon Lt Col
                            Wm Prescott Col.
                            Ephm Corey Leiut,
                            Joseph Baker Lieut.
                            Joshua Row Lieut.

To The Honorable General Court of the
Massachusetts Bay.

Jonas Richardson Capt
Eliphalet Bodwell Sergt
Josiah — Neele... Leiut
Ebenr Varnum ...Leiut
Wm Hudson Ballard Ct

William Smith Capt
John Morton Sergt. of a the....
Lieut. Richard Welsh

In Council Decr 21. 1775
Read & Sent Down   Perez Morton Dpty Secry

Recommendation of
Salem Poor a free
Negro...
...
...
...
read & concurd...

4

"That All Men Are Created Equal . . ."

★ ★ ★

THE AMERICAN REVOLUTION

Boston had become a dangerous place. British soldiers were quartered in houses all throughout the city. The siege surrounded the city. Now, the Battle of Bunker Hill had been fought. Many colonists who sided with the patriots fled to safety.

Phillis Wheatley left her home on King Street, and traveled to Providence, Rhode Island. Most likely, she lived with Mary Wheatley, the patriot daughter of loyalists John and Susanna Wheatley. Once in Rhode Island, Phillis Wheatley was also near her close correspondent and friend, Obour Tanner. Letters that Phillis wrote to her still survive and are a wonderful way to catch a glimpse into the mind and heart of this amazing poet.

While in Providence, Phillis Wheatley wrote a letter to George Washington, who had set up his headquarters near Boston in Cambridge, Massachusetts. Along with her letter, Wheatley included a poem that she had written in Washington's honor.

Surprised by the excellent quality of the poem as well as gratified by her praise, George Washington wrote back to Wheatley. He invited her to visit him. Within a month, both her letter and her poem were printed by Thomas Paine in the *Pennsylvania Magazine*. Wheatley later traveled to Cambridge where she visited with Washington.

Wheatley stayed in Providence until the British evacuated Boston in March of 1776. When the city appeared safe again, she returned to Boston.

The Bucks of America

The Bucks of America were an all-black unit during the Revolutionary War. Thought to be commanded by the famous abolitionist Colonel George Middleton of Boston, some historians say this military unit was probably formed to protect the patriot colonists in Boston.

Governor John Hancock and his son invited the unit to stop on Beacon Street in front of the governor's mansion. Colonel Middleton and the Bucks of America were presented with a beautiful silk flag "as a tribute to their courage and devotion throughout the struggle." The flag bore the emblem of their unit, a buck, or deer, standing tall and proud beneath a tree.

It is not known whether Prince Hall, leader of Boston's free black community, enlisted in the Bucks of America or fought in the American Revolution. There were several men named Prince Hall who appeared on various muster rolls, but historians are not quite sure which one, if any, were Prince Hall, the founder of black Freemasonry. The same year during the war that Prince Hall signed and submitted a petition for the end of slavery, however, he also wrote up a bill of sale for leather drumheads. As a leather dresser and owner of the leather goods shop called the Golden Fleece, Prince Hall supplied these drumheads to the Boston Regiment of Artillery.

Bucks of America flag.
Oil paint on silk, circa 1776.
Courtesy of the Massachusetts Historical Society

Bill of sale for five drumheads from Prince Hall to the Regiment of Artillery.

Courtesy of Massachusetts Archives

Lord Dunmore's Proclamation

On November 7, 1775, British Governor Lord Dunmore issued a proclamation inviting those who were enslaved to run away and join the British army. All throughout the South, great numbers of slaves escaped to fight as Loyalists. Some became soldiers, while some became spies. Others joined the navy. Lord Dunmore's Ethiopian Regiment was formed and fought bravely until smallpox killed many.

Dunmore's proclamation shocked colonial leaders. Up to this point, they had not allowed African Americans to join the Continental Army, even though numerous black patriots had already enlisted in their local militias. Now colonial leaders realized that they would soon be outnumbered by British troops who had the enlisted support of former slaves. A decision was finally made to allow African Americans to enlist.

A New Center of Government

While Boston was a center of patriot protest during the beginning stages of the American Revolution, another city, Philadelphia, became the center for the organization of the new colonial government. Independence Hall, known then as the State House, was located in Philadelphia. The Liberty Bell, known at that time as the State House Bell, rang out constantly, alerting the citizens of Philadelphia about important and historic events.

The Continental Congress began meeting at Independence Hall in Philadelphia as early as 1774. Delegates arrived on horseback or in carriages, clattering over cobblestone streets on their way to meetings. Representatives from all 13 colonies assembled there to discuss their plan of action against the tyranny of British rule.

In Independence Hall and throughout the streets of Philadelphia, freedom was dawning. Free blacks and enslaved individuals lived on every street, often side-by-side with fellow

Design a Flag

During the American Revolution, different units carried their own flags. The Bucks of America were honored with a silk flag displaying their emblem of a buck, or deer, standing proudly under a tree. The First Rhode Island Regiment carried a flag with the emblem of a blue anchor against a background of white along with yellow stars against a background of blue. You can design your own flag.

Materials

★ Cotton pillowcase, white or cream, or old cotton sheet cut the same size as a pillowcase

★ Pencil and scratch paper

★ Fabric markers or fabric paint

★ Fabric scraps

★ Needle and thread

★ ¾-inch wooden dowel rod to use as a standard flag-pole, or a small decorative metal flagpole to plant in the ground (optional)

1. Pre-wash the cotton fabric if it hasn't yet been washed.

2. Decide which type of flagpole you will use to display your flag. Determine whether your flag will hang from the side or from the top.

3. Draw a design on scratch paper that you would like to use to decorate your flag.

4. When you are satisfied with the design, draw the picture lightly on the fabric with your pencil.

5. Using a protected work surface, paint the design on the fabric with fabric markers or paint. Allow to dry.

6. If you plan to display your flag on a flagpole, use fabric scraps to sew tabs on your flag to slide over the flag pole.

white patriots. All throughout Philadelphia, African Americans worked in the taverns, inns, and coffeehouses where heated discussions took place about the natural rights and liberties people were entitled to have. African Americans heard them. Well-known patriots of the day printed radical pamphlets calling for justice and equal rights. African Americans read them. Newspaper articles stated passionate opinions against the English crown's attempts to treat the colonies like slaves. African Americans discussed them. Throughout the city, the free and enslaved black population was caught up in the historic tide of events.

During these years, many of the delegates who arrived to attend the Continental Congress brought personal attendants. Most of these were enslaved. When these slaves witnessed the patriotic zeal and freedoms Philadelphia's African American community experienced, many were no longer able to bear the thought of returning home.

Philadelphia's Young Patriot

Just down the street from Independence Hall lived a very young patriot named James Forten. His home was in an area of Philadelphia known as Dock Ward, located near the corner of Third and Walnut Streets.

Young James Forten enjoyed playing games of marbles. As he and his friends played marbles just outside his house, the tall tower of Independence Hall could be glimpsed through the trees.

One hot summer July day in 1776, nine-year-old James Forten heard the Liberty Bell, or State House Bell, ring out loud and clear. James dropped what he was doing and ran down the street. He headed straight to Independence Hall. A large, noisy crowd was gathering outside.

Just then, an important-looking man held up a paper. After it was quiet, the man began to read.

Young James Forten was in the crowd at Independence Hall in Philadelphia on July 8, 1776, where he heard the first public reading of the Declaration of Independence.
Courtesy of the Library of Congress, Prints & Photographs Division, LC-USZ62-112159

Read the Declaration

When he was nine years old, it thrilled James Forten to hear the Declaration of Independence read aloud. You can experience the same thrill and excitement by reading this historic document aloud with your friends.

If you don't already have a copy of the Declaration of Independence, you can print one out by visiting the Web site "The Declaration of Independence" at www.ushistory.org/Declaration/.

Sit down with your friends, explore the site, look at the original image of the handwritten document, and print out a copy of the text. First read through the text together and underline words you don't know. Look up those words in a dictionary. Then assign parts to read aloud by dividing the document into small sections for each one of your friends to read.

Finally, practice reading the entire document aloud by having each of your friends read his assigned part. Then read the document aloud to your family, friends, or class.

When in the Course of human events it becomes necessary for one people to dissolve the political bands which have connected them with another and to assume among the powers of the earth, the separate and equal station to which the Laws of Nature and of Nature's God entitle them, a decent respect to the opinions of mankind requires that they should declare the causes which impel them to the separation.

We hold these truths to be self-evident, that all men are created equal, that they are endowed by their Creator with certain unalienable Rights, that among these are Life, Liberty and the pursuit of Happiness.

James was moved in a deep way by these very powerful words. As he stood in the crowd, it was a moment he would never forget. He believed in the words declaring the importance of hope, freedom, and liberty for all. Many years later, he often recalled how his heart stirred to hear this document read.

James Forten's Adventures at Sea

When James Forten was 14 years old, he decided to join the Continental Navy on a privateer called the *Royal Louis*. A privateer was a privately owned boat that was officially signed on to be part of the new navy. These privateers patrolled the waters, searching for British ships.

Forten was assigned the job of a powder boy, as were most youths who joined the navy. Because it was dangerous to keep the powder on deck near the cannons where it might explode from the flames, the powder was kept below deck. In the thick of the fighting, Forten had to run below deck, grab a supply of powder, and then carry it up to give to the men to shoot the cannons.

The *Royal Louis* was a stout fighter. But when it met up with British warships one day, it didn't stand a chance. The privateer was captured. Plans were made to sell Forten and the other African American crewmen as slaves, even though he had been born free and was never a slave. The British waited for a ship to sail past that could take Forten and the black prisoners south.

While they waited, however, Forten became friends with the British captain's son. Forten taught his new friend how to play marbles. When the ship finally arrived to take him south into slavery, his new friend protested so much that Forten was not sold.

Instead, Forten and the other prisoners were put on board a British prison ship named the *Jersey*. There were a number of these prison ships anchored off the coast. All of them were terrible, dirty places where the British kept prisoners of war.

Located in the New York harbor, the *Jersey* was one of the worst prison ships of all. Many prisoners died, but not Forten. After seven long months floating aboard the *Jersey*, he was

The prison ship *Jersey*.
Courtesy of the Peabody Essex Museum, Salem, Massachusetts

released. He went back to his home in Philadelphia and got a job working as a sailmaker. He eventually became one of the wealthiest and most influential men in Philadelphia.

The Continental Navy

James Forten was just one of many African American sailors who joined the Continental Navy. Many shipped with crews on privateers. Others signed up to join one of the states that organized a navy. States such as Massachusetts and Connecticut recruited both white and black patriots, free and enslaved, in their navy. Other states, such as Virginia and South Carolina, enlisted enslaved men to sail as well.

Like Forten's, Paul Cuffe's ship was captured by the British during the Revolutionary

War. Like Forten, Cuffe was imprisoned on a prison ship floating in the New York Harbor. And just like Forten, Cuffe left his mark on history through the petitions he signed crying out for liberty and equal rights. After the end of the American Revolution, Cuffe went on to gain fame as a wealthy ship's captain.

African Americans took part in many of the battles at sea, including one of the most famous of all—John Paul Jones' ship the *Bonhomme Richard* against the British ship *Seraphis*. Men such as Cato Carlile, Scipio Africanus, and Paul Jones fought and served under John Paul Jones. Some historians point out that at least one of these men, Paul Jones, took part in the fighting aboard the *Bonhomme Richard* during its epic battle.

African American sailors such as Paul Jones took part in the fighting aboard the *Bonhomme Richard* during its epic battle against the British ship *Serapis*.
Courtesy National Archives (148-GW-444)

Crossing the Delaware

On a blustery winter's night, the Continental Army made a daring move. It was Christmas, December 25, 1776. Nobody thought the army would do anything except relax around warm campfires. Nobody thought the patriot troops would march out on such a cold, freezing night. They were wrong. The Hessians, German soldiers hired by England to fight against the colonists, were celebrating Christmas in Trenton that day. Counting on this, the Continental Army set out to take them by surprise.

Men such as Oliver Cromwell were there with Washington's historic campaign. Oliver Cromwell crossed the Delaware River with the other men in his unit. He marched through the freezing ice and snow toward Trenton. He fought against the Hessian soldiers and rejoiced in the amazing and astounding victory.

To The Honourable Councel and House of Representatives in General Court assembled for the State of the massachusetts Bay in New England March 14th AD 1780

The Petition of Several poor Negroes & molattoes who are Inhabitants of the Town of Dartmouth Humbly Sheweth —

That we being Chiefly of the African Extract and by Reason of Long Bondage and hard Slavery we have been deprived of Enjoying the Profits of our Labour or the advantage of Inheriting Estates from our Parents as our Neighbours the white people do having some of us not long Injoyed our own freedom yet of late Contrary to the invariable Custom & Practice of the Country we have been & now are Taxed both in our Polls and that small Distance of Estate which through much hard Labour & Industry we have got together to Sustain our selves & families withall — We apprehend it therefore to be hard usaage and will doubtless if Continued will Reduce us to a State of Beggary whereby we shall become a Burthen to others if not timely prevented by the Interposition of your Justice & power yor petitioners father Sheweth that we apprehend our selves to be Aggrieved, in that while we are not allowed the Privilage of freemen of the State having no vote or Influence in the Election of those that Tax us yet many of our Colour (as is will known) have Cheerfully Entered the field of Battle in the defence of the Common Cause and that (as we Conceive) against a similar Exertion of power (in Regard to Taxation) too well known to need a Recital in this place

that these the

Most honourable Court we Humbley Beseech they to take this into Consideration and let us aside from Paying tax or taxes or Cause us to be Cleared for we Ever have Been a people that Was far from all these thing Ever Since the Days of our four fathers and therefore we take it as a head ship that we should Be so Rated by men in these Difficulty times for their felt By nor in these Difficulty times for there is not Severel more then five or six that hath tooke a Cow in this town and therefore in our Distress we send unto the the most Honourable Court for Releif under the peaceabelnefs of thee people and the mercy of God that we may Be Releaved for we are not alowed in voating in the town meeting in nor to Chuse a officer or either their Was not one Ever heard in the active Court of the General asembly in nor for the poor Distsefd miserable Black people & we have not an Equial Chance with white peaoule either By Sea nor By Land therefore we take it as a head ship that poor old negros should Be Rated which have Been in Bondage Some thirty Some forty Some fifty years and now just got their Liberty Some by goung into the Servise and Some By going to Sea and others By good forian and also poor Distsefses mungrels which have no larning and no Land and also no Stock either where to Put their head but Some Shelter them Selves into an old rotten hut which they Logs a could not Lay in

therefore we pray that they may give no offense at all nor By no means But that thee most Honourable Court will take it in to Consideration as if it were their own case for we think it all to Be a head ship that we Should Be afsessed and not Be a Losed as we may say to Eat Bread therefore we Humbley Beg and pray thee to plead our Case for us or with thy people o god that those who have the Rule in their hands may Be merrysfull unto the poor and needy give unto those who ask of the or he that would Borrow of thee turn thou not away Empty o god Be merrysfull unto the poor and give unto those who give ought unto the poor therefore we Return unto thee again most honourable Court that thou wouldst Consider us in these Distsenite times that we Send in nor Come unto the with false words for we Send in nor Come unto the with being Lyes there fore we think neither with being Lyes there fore we think that we may Be Clear from Being Called Lories the Some of our Colour hath Rebelied and Dare Wickedly hove Ever we think that their is more of our Collour gone into the wars according to the number of them into the Respicktive towns then any other nation here and here away therefore We Most Humbley Request therefor that you would take our Unhappy Case into your Serious Consideration and in your Wisdom and Power Grant us Releif from Taxation while under our Present Deprefsed Circumstances and your poor Petitioners as in duty Bound Shall Ever pray &c

Dated at Dartmouth the 10th of February 5780

John Cuffe
Adventer Child &c

Always by Washington's side, William Lee was with the commander in chief at the historic crossing of the Delaware River.

Courtesy of the Library of Congress, Prints & Photographs Division, LC-USZ62-5850

Servant Soldier

Although not listed on the muster roll of the Continental Army, another African American named William Lee participated in the historic crossing of the Delaware River. Lee was George Washington's personal valet and servant. Enslaved since birth, he was purchased by Washington when he was about 17 years old. Lee moved to Mount Vernon, where he became a house servant and the personal attendant to the future president.

During every event of the American Revolution, Lee was by George Washington's side. A fine horseman, he rode into battle next to Washington, ready to help the commander in chief. From the Siege of Boston to Valley Forge to the final victory at Yorktown, Lee was an eyewitness to the American Revolution.

Valley Forge

Perhaps one of the most well-known events during the American Revolution was the winter encampment at Valley Forge. It's common knowledge that George Washington settled his troops here to keep an eye on the British during their winter stay in Philadelphia. But what many do not know is that a significant number of the troops at Valley Forge were African Americans.

The muster roll lists Oliver Cromwell from the Second New Jersey Regiment as arriving with the troops at Valley Forge in December. William Lee accompanied George Washington to Valley Forge. Peter Salem was here. He had been part of the fighting since the very first day when British troops marched into Concord. He was credited by many to have shot and killed British Major Pitcairn at the Battle of Bunker Hill. Salem Poor was also at Valley Forge. Honored as the most famous soldier at the Battle of Bunker Hill, 14 officers signed a petition commending his brave and heroic deeds on that historic day. Now he was at Valley Forge, starving with the others when they often had only "firecakes" to eat.

Oliver Cromwell (1753–1853)

For over six years of dedicated and heroic service in the Continental Army, Oliver Cromwell received an honorable discharge with a Badge of Merit. Enlisted as a freeman with the Second New Jersey Regiment, Cromwell had

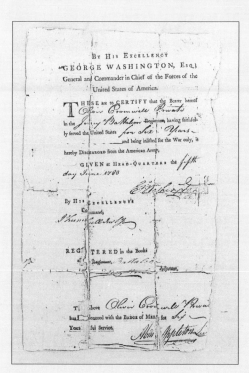

marched with the troops on the historic Christmas crossing of the Delaware River. He was at the battles of Trenton, Princeton, Brandywine, and Monmouth. At Yorktown, he witnessed the very last soldier killed in the very last battle of the American Revolution. When Cromwell was discharged at the end of the war, Commander in Chief George Washington signed his papers himself.

Oliver Cromwell's discharge papers and the Badge of Merit, signed by Commander in Chief George Washington.
Courtesy National Archives (NWCT-1R)

Bake Firecakes

Perfect for making at a campout, firecakes can be baked on a flat rock over the campfire. If you want to make them at home, you can bake them on a cookie sheet. Have an adult help you.

Adult supervision required

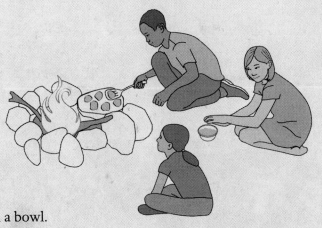

Ingredients

★ 3 cups flour

★ 1 cup water

★ salt

Makes 6–8 firecakes

1. Mix the flour, water, and a pinch of salt in a bowl.

2. Grab a ball of dough, flatten it like a pancake in the palm of your hand, and place it on a flat rock over the campfire. Make 6 to 8 firecakes from the dough. Or bake them on a cookie sheet in the oven at 425°F until brown.

An Extraordinary Soldier

On the muster roll at Valley Forge, one man's name had a special note written next to it. "Extraordinary Pay February 16, 1778" was handwritten on the pay roll for Nero Hawley. The details aren't known, but we can assume that he was an extraordinary soldier in order to have received this special award.

Enlisted in the Second Connecticut with several other African Americans from his hometown of Stratford, Hawley signed up in April 1777. A month before the encampment, his regiment was ordered to join Washington's army for the winter.

Hawley marched into Valley Forge with the Continental Army on the evening of December 19, 1777. He helped build sturdy wooden huts. He was used to working with logs. A slave, he worked at the local sawmill in Stratford.

At Valley Forge, Hawley's duties were listed as scout. He helped keep a careful eye on the British so the Redcoats didn't travel throughout the countryside destroying farmland or terrorizing families.

After the Second Connecticut marched out of Valley Forge in the spring, records show that Hawley continued to serve in various battles and campaigns. During the next winter, he became sick and was hospitalized, as were many of the other soldiers. Discharged due to illness, he returned home to his wife and children.

Hawley was finally set free in 1782. He was also able to buy the freedom of several of his children. He purchased land, established a home, and started his own brickmaking business.

The Support Camp

It took 400 barrels of flour and 800 beef cows to feed 11,000 troops at Valley Forge each week. A support camp was set up where soldiers came for their rations. Livestock such as cows, pigs, and sheep were kept in pens. Ovens were built into small hillsides where bread was baked. Local men and women were hired to cook and help feed the troops.

Cyrus Bustill was a baker who helped supply bread at Valley Forge. According to family tradition, he received a silver coin from George Washington in commemoration of his service. After the American Revolution, Bustill went on to become one of the foremost African American leaders in the city of Philadelphia. He and his family were prominent abolitionists, and his descendants included such greats as artist Robert Douglass Jr. and world-famous actor Paul Robeson.

(left) Hut at Valley Forge.
Courtesy of Jordan Sangerman

(right) Oven at Valley Forge.
Courtesy of Jordan Sangerman

Nero Hawley

This extraordinary patriot received one month of "extraordinary pay" during his stay at Valley Forge. At a time when men were starving, morale was low, and many soldiers died from exposure and disease, Hawley's exemplary actions earned him a special reward. He was not one of the countless deserters or one of the men who secretly planned a mutiny. He served the Continental Army faithfully at Valley Forge, and was paid extra for his dedication and hard work.

Explore Your Family Tree

Many people are discovering today that their ancestors fought in the American Revolution. The search has become much easier with new online services. For instance, if you know the name of an ancestor who lived in the colonies during the era of the Revolutionary War, you can search for his name at www.valleyforgemusterroll.org to see if he spent the winter at Valley Forge.

First visit the home page. Then click on the link for the muster roll. Next type in your ancestor's last name. Also type in the abbreviation for the state he lived in. See if any soldiers were listed with your ancestor's name. If so, follow the links to find out more information about that soldier.

If you don't know the names of any ancestors who lived during the era of the Revolutionary War, start your search by exploring your family tree. There are different shapes you can make your tree. One is a Stacking Triangles Tree.

Materials

* ★ Unlined paper
* ★ Scissors
* ★ Ruler
* ★ Pencil
* ★ Clear tape
* ★ Poster board

1. Cut out 8-inch triangles from the blank paper. Use the diagram shown to draw a horizontal line across the middle of the triangle. (Line 1) Now draw a vertical line to divide that triangle into two parts. (Line 2) Write the name of your father in the left half and the name of your mother in the right half. Next draw lines in the bottom half to make enough spaces for each of your brothers and sisters. Be sure to include a space for you. (Lines 3 and 4) Write each of your names in one of the spaces. This triangle is the bottom of your Stacking Triangles Tree. Tape it to the bottom center of the poster board.

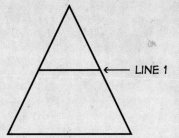
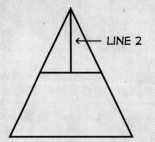
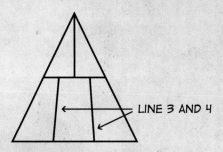

2. Divide a second triangle in a similar manner to represent your father's side of the family. Write your grandfather's name in the top left and your grandmother's name in the top right. Write the names of your father and his brothers and sisters in the spaces on the bottom half of the triangle. Tape this triangle above the first one.

3. Continue to follow your father's line of male or female ancestors back as far as you can go by making a triangle for each generation as shown. Ask your parents or other relatives for help gathering information.

4. Make a similar Stacking Triangles Tree for your mother's side of the family.

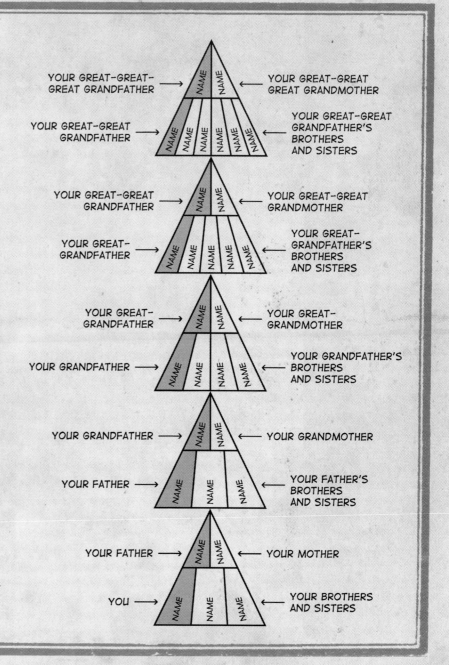

Cook Pepper Pot Soup

When rations were low, George Washington requested a hearty dish for his troops. The cook filled a pot with peppercorns, scraps of leftovers, and a meat called tripe made from the stomach of a cow. Everything was simmered together to produce this flavorful soup.

Adult supervision required

Ingredients

★ ¼ cup plus ⅓ cup butter

★ 1 onion, sliced

★ 2 sticks celery, chopped

★ 2 carrots, sliced

★ 1 green pepper, chopped

★ 3 ½ tablespoons flour

★ 5 cups chicken stock

Serves 4 to 6

★ 3 medium potatoes, cubed

★ ½ lb. honeycomb tripe, cut into cubes (You could also use beef, lamb, chicken, or a mixture of meats.)

★ ½ teaspoon peppercorns, finely pounded

★ ¾ teaspoon salt

★ garlic and chili pepper to taste

★ ½ cup evaporated milk or heavy cream

1. In large soup kettle, sauté onion, celery, carrots, and green pepper in ¼ cup butter until soft.

2. Stir in flour until well mixed.

3. Add remaining ingredients except cream and remaining butter.

4. Cover and simmer for 1½ hours.

5. Just before serving, stir in cream and butter.

Wagons of Salt

During the American Revolution, salt was a valuable item. Without salt, the troops couldn't prevent their meat from going rotten. Without salt, the few provisions they had wouldn't last.

Various saltworks operated throughout the colonies. Salt was made from boiling fresh ocean water until it evaporated, leaving the salt crystals behind. Men were hired to drive wagonloads of salt inland to the troops.

The British understood the army's vital need for salt. They frequently attacked the supply wagons and stole the salt. The job of a salt wagon driver was a very dangerous, yet very important, contribution to the success of the Continental Army.

Young Richard Allen signed up to drive salt from Rehoboth, Delaware, inland to the troops. Some accounts say he drove salt to Valley Forge. It was dangerous, yet he believed he was doing much, much more than taking salt to help feed hungry men. He also believed he was spending his time helping to feed people's souls.

Allen used this season as a salt wagon driver to try to help fill the need for religious teaching. He became a traveling preacher and stopped frequently so that he could preach and pray with people along his route. The long hours he spent driving his team of horses gave him time to meditate upon the Bible. Hour after hour spent alone on the road also gave him time to pray.

Illness and Disease

Not only did the men suffer from cold and starvation during the winter at Valley Forge, but illness and disease spread through the ranks. Pneumonia, dysentery, typhus, and "the itch" accounted for much sickness and even death. In spring, many soldiers came down with smallpox, including Cato Baker, who had enlisted with the Second New Hampshire Regiment.

Writing home to an acquaintance, Baker describes conditions in the Continental Army. "I had the small pox in Valley Forge last March," he wrote, "but now I am of good health." In his letter, he also explained that the usual rations included one pound of beef, one pound of bread, and one gill (a quarter of a pint) of rum every other day. This letter, and a second one Baker wrote, give us a more complete picture of the African American presence in the Revolutionary War.

Make Homemade Salt

One way that salt has been produced is by solar evaporation. Ocean water is diverted into shallow pools or ponds where the sun evaporates the water, leaving crystals of salt behind. You can make your own salt, too.

Materials

★ Table salt

★ Old metal cake pan

★ Measuring cups

★ Whisk

1. Add ⅛ cup of table salt to 2 cups of tap water. Stir with a whisk until the salt is dissolved.

2. Pour some of the water into an old, clean metal cake pan—just enough to cover the bottom of the pan.

3. Set the pan in a sunny spot and allow the water to evaporate. This process may take several days.

4. After the water evaporates, scrape the salt out of the pan. Use the large crystals in cooking, or serve with a meal! (Note: If you make salt from ocean water instead of tap water, the salt might have germs in it, and should not be eaten unless it undergoes a purification process.)

The Rhode Island Regiment

Conditions were desperate in the Continental Army at Valley Forge. So many men deserted the ranks that George Washington sent out a call for more troops.

In Rhode Island, they were unable to recruit enough white volunteers to meet their quota. The state government, therefore, issued a statement in January 1778 that any slave who volunteered would be given his freedom and receive the same pay as other soldiers.

The response was immediate. Over 200 African Americans enlisted in the First Rhode Island Regiment, many of them former slaves. The men signed up to fight for the duration of the war. Once assembled, the troops marched to join Valley Forge.

Together with the other men, these new soldiers drilled and trained under the new leadership of Baron von Steuben, the Prussian commander endorsed by France who arrived at Valley Forge in the spring.

After the Continental Army left Valley Forge on June 19, 1778, the First Rhode Island Regiment went on to prove their skill in battle. Eyewitness accounts of the Battle of Rhode Island, as well as other battles and campaigns, tell of these courageous men. The First Rhode Island Regiment held their ground amid heavy fire, advanced to overtake British and Hessian troops, and fought with bravery and zeal.

The Invisible Spy

The American Revolution continued for years. During the summer of 1781, the British Army marched to Virginia and settled into Yorktown.

Virginia was home to an enslaved man named James Armistead. During these difficult years, he had accompanied his owner, a military supply officer, as a personal servant. During the summer of 1781, Armistead heard that the young French general, the Marquis de Lafayette, was in need of spies.

Armistead was a daring and educated man. Before the war, it was his job to perform important duties as a clerk in his owner's offices in Richmond, Virginia. Now he stepped forward and volunteered his service. It would be a dangerous assignment, but he was willing to risk his life for the freedoms he longed for so deeply.

At first Lafayette assigned Armistead the task of spying on Benedict Arnold. When Arnold moved north, however, Armistead's new assignment was to spy on the British troops in Yorktown.

British soldiers didn't suspect Armistead was a spy when he suddenly appeared in

African American artilleryman in the Continental Army.

Used with Permission of Documenting the American South, the University of North Carolina at Chapel Hill Libraries

James Armistead Lafayette (c. 1748–1830)

Intelligent. Brave. Daring. Working as a double agent for the Continental Army, James Armistead was all this—and more. He volunteered to be a spy when he learned that Lafayette needed informants to go behind British lines in Virginia. First sent to spy on Benedict Arnold, Armistead's next assignment was to spy on Cornwallis. Once in Cornwallis's tents, Armistead tricked Cornwallis into believing that he would spy for the British—all the while telling Lafayette of Cornwallis's every plan. This dangerous and secretive strategy contributed to the Americans winning the war.

James Armistead is an American hero. After the war, he took the last name of Lafayette. He petitioned the court of Virginia and was awarded his freedom. He received a pension during old age. When Lafayette returned to tour the United States in 1824, the French general wrote James Armistead Lafayette a glowing letter of recommendation.

James Armistead
Courtesy National Archives (19-N-1583)

camp. Ever since Lord Dunmore's proclamation, many local slaves ran away and joined British troops.

Armistead knew he would need to gain the trust of the British, however. At first, he performed manual duties like many of the other runaway slaves. He often went out with other men to search for available food in local fields, farms, or communities.

Much more cultured and intelligent than an uneducated field hand, however, Armistead did not go unnoticed. Soon he was appointed to serve Lord Cornwallis. In the general's tents, Armistead worked among the officers and assisted them with their daily needs. The officers talked freely in front of him, hardly even noticing who stood in the shadows of the tent while they made important plans. It was as if he were invisible, which suited his purpose and mission perfectly.

But now, Armistead's job became even more risky. He volunteered his services as a spy to Lord Cornwallis. Now he was acting as a double agent! While pretending to be a spy for Cornwallis, he was actually a spy for Lafayette.

Armistead sent a steady supply of important and valuable information to Lafayette. Lafayette, in turn, passed on these details to George Washington. With this information, Washington made plans for the French fleet and the Continental Army to trap Cornwallis.

Washington's plans were a grand success, thanks to the timely information Armistead provided. The Continental Army surrounded the British on land, and French fleets cut off their escape by sea. After days of intense fighting, the British finally surrendered. On October 19, 1781, George Washington signed the official surrender from Cornwallis, and the Revolutionary War came to an end. The colonists had finally won, thanks to the very important espionage work of James Armistead.

With information secretly obtained by Armistead, patriots trapped the British at Yorktown and forced their surrender. This cartoon shows the American snake with its coils surrounding the British troops at Yorktown, Virginia.

Courtesy of the Library of Congress, Prints & Photographs Division, LC-USZ62-1531

A Glorious Victory

The Battle of Yorktown had been a glorious victory. The Rhode Island Regiment was there and fought bravely among the troops. Oliver Cromwell reported that at the end of the battle, he saw the last British soldier killed in the war. Peter Salem was there, having seen action since the very first day of the war. As always, William Lee was there, riding his horse at the side of George Washington. Many other African American soldiers fought gallantly at this final battle as well.

On October 19, 1781, a solemn assembly was held at Yorktown where the British surrendered to the Americans. Cornwallis's sword was symbolically handed over to Washington. Later, a marvelous parade highlighted the victory celebrations while colonial troops marched proudly in review. Of that day, one observer wrote in his diary that the First Rhode Island Regiment was the "most neatly

African American horseman at the Surrender of Yorktown, probably William Lee.

Courtesy of the Library of Congress, Prints & Photographs Division, LC-USZ62-45

dressed, the best under arms, and the most precise in its maneuvers."

The Treaty of Paris was signed on September 3, 1783—the colonists were no longer under British rule. They were Americans now, and a new nation was born. Over 5,000 African Americans had joined in the six long years of fighting. Black patriots such as Massachusetts minutemen Samuel Craft of Newton, Isaiah Bayoman of Stoneham, and Cato Stedman and Cuff Whitemore of Cambridge, fought from the very first day at Lexington and Concord, through the Battle of Bunker Hill, and in every major battle of the war. Some men, like Prince Whipple, Primas Hall, and Agrippa Hull, served as personal attendants of officers while also participating actively on numerous military campaigns.

Others, such as Pompey Lamb, were spies, and risked their lives to carry vital information across enemy lines. Some of the soldiers, like Richard Cozzens, a fifer in the First Rhode Island Regiment, had been born in Africa and survived the Middle Passage before joining the Continental Army.

Many African Americans fought side by side among their neighbors. Others fought in mostly all-black units, including the Volunteer Chasseurs from faraway Haiti who traveled across land and sea to join in the cause for liberty. Others, such as Richard Allen, drove supplies or worked hard to meet the daily needs of the troops. These brave heroes sacrificed and suffered with the army and the navy for the duration of the war up through the glorious victory at Yorktown, Virginia.

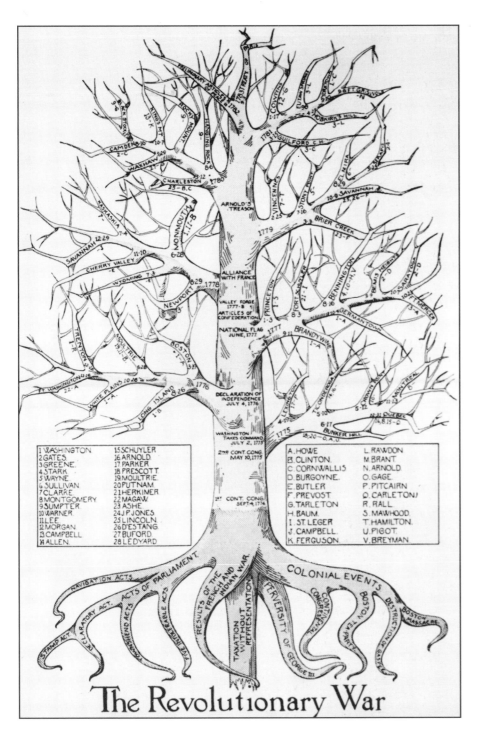

African American patriots fought in every major battle of the American Revolution.

Courtesy National Archives (148-GW-378)

5

"That They Are Endowed by Their Creator with Certain Unalienable Rights..."

★ ★ ★

AFRICAN AMERICANS AS CITIZENS

The American Revolution was over. In the struggle to claim their basic rights, the colonists had fought bravely and won. For young Richard Allen, it was a brand new day. Not only was his nation free, he was a free man. His passion and goal was now to preach. He traveled throughout the neighborhood of Wilmington, Delaware, and then to New Jersey. During the days, Allen worked hard cutting wood to earn his living. At night and on Sundays, he ministered to families and neighbors.

For 24-year-old Allen, this was a very difficult time. He suffered from bouts of fever, pleurisy, and rheumatism. Travel was not easy during that era. Roads could be deep muddy trenches or frozen and slippery. Allen walked from place to place. At one point his feet were so sore that after he sat down to have tea, he could not stand up again. His host bathed Allen's feet with water and bran, and the next day he felt better.

This was a very rewarding time for Allen, however. He met the minister Benjamin Abbot. Even though he was of a different race and background, Allen considered Abbot to be both friend and father. In each new neighborhood he also found people, both black and white, who were eager to hear about his faith.

Circuit Preacher

By now, large congregations were gathering to hear Richard Allen. He traveled to Pennsylvania and Maryland. Often, he was invited to stay for days and weeks at a time.

In the early 1780s, ministers traveled from community to community, assigned to visit certain neighborhoods. These assignments were known as "circuits." Soon, Allen was invited to travel with ministers in Connecticut along the Hartford Circuit and then in Maryland on the Baltimore Circuit.

Allen received an invitation to travel along with a white minister throughout the southern states. It was a difficult decision for him. He would not be allowed to talk with the

> "After peace was proclaimed I then traveled extensively, striving to preach the Gospel."
>
> —Richard Allen

> "I preached for them the next evening. We had a glorious meeting." —Richard Allen

slaves. And he could be kidnapped and sold back into slavery.

It was an offer Allen could not take. He had fought too hard for freedom. Instead, he began to travel the Lancaster Circuit in Pennsylvania. Now he was preaching near the city of Philadelphia. Since he was so near the city and was so popular, the elder in charge of the congregation in Philadelphia invited him frequently to come and minister.

Religious Revival

In the years leading up to the American Revolution, religious revival had swept through the colonies. Camp meetings were held and new churches formed. Richard Allen was part of this movement now called the Great Awakening.

After the Revolutionary War was over, another religious revival took place called the Second Great Awakening. Camp meetings were central to its success. Denominations split. New churches were formed. Circuit preachers traveled from community to community, speaking to eager crowds.

Great African American preachers emerged. John Marrant was ordained as a Methodist minister and later appointed chaplain of the Masonic Lodge in Boston. Lemuel Haynes pastored a church in Vermont for 30 years. One of his sermons was published and reprinted 70 times.

In North Carolina, freeborn and college-educated John Chavis set about to preach as well as teach. He traveled by horseback throughout North Carolina, Virginia, and Maryland for nearly 30 years, speaking to crowds of free blacks and slaves as well as large audiences of whites. During his career as a missionary, he also opened a school for children of both black and white families. Offering classes in Latin, Greek, and college preparatory subjects, many of his students went on to become noteworthy citizens and government leaders.

One of the greatest orators of this age was Harry Hosier. He was a circuit-rider for the early Methodist Church. Records show that Hosier began his public career in 1780. By then, he was no longer a slave. He traveled all along the Atlantic coastline and accompanied many well-known Methodist ministers. His role was to assist these men, drive the horses, and minister to slaves and free black congregations.

It was soon evident that Hosier was much more than an ordinary assistant. His oratory skills were so eloquent and his personality was so magnificent that large crowds of people, both black and white, gathered to hear him

John Chavis (1763-1838)

John Chavis was a man of letters. He attended what is now known as Princeton University. A student of Greek and Latin, he also studied the Bible. During his 30-year career as a teacher and missionary, he became well-known throughout several southern states. He established a school. Many of his students became distinguished and notable citizens.

"Envy and pride are the leading lines to all the misery that mankind has suffered from the beginning of the world to this day."
—John Marrant

speak. He could memorize scriptures from the Bible with amazing skill. He remembered verses from hymns with amazing accuracy. Many colonial leaders claimed Hosier was the greatest speaker of their time.

In 1784, the Methodist Episcopal Church was established as an official denomination. Because of Hosier's powerful influence in the church, many African Americans joined the new denomination. In 1796, Hosier went on to help establish the Zoar Methodist Church in Philadelphia, Pennsylvania, one of the oldest black congregations in America.

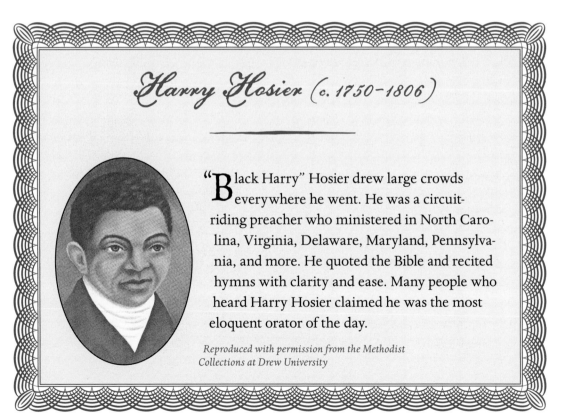

Harry Hosier (c. 1750–1806)

"Black Harry" Hosier drew large crowds everywhere he went. He was a circuit-riding preacher who ministered in North Carolina, Virginia, Delaware, Maryland, Pennsylvania, and more. He quoted the Bible and recited hymns with clarity and ease. Many people who heard Harry Hosier claimed he was the most eloquent orator of the day.

Reproduced with permission from the Methodist Collections at Drew University

Philadelphia

In 1786 Richard Allen had been traveling and preaching near Philadelphia on the Lancaster Circuit. He received an invitation from St. George's Church in Philadelphia to come and preach.

While he ministered at St. George and different gatherings throughout the city, he realized that Philadelphia was quickly becoming home to a large community of free blacks. Everywhere he went he found growing pockets of African Americans, most of them newly freed, uneducated, and without a clear purpose in life.

> *"It was not uncommon for me to preach from four to five times a day."* —Richard Allen

Philadelphia was growing. By 1800, it would be the largest city in the nation. Because of its geographical location, Philadelphia was a transportation hub. It was a busy port. It was the first northern city on the eastern seaboard where most travelers arrived after leaving the slave states to the south. Since 1780, a law had been passed for gradual emancipation in Pennsylvania. Often, runaway slaves from the South made Philadelphia their destination.

Everywhere Richard Allen went throughout the city of Philadelphia, he found people in need of leadership, spiritual guidance, and economic assistance. His heart was stirred. He established prayer meetings. He formed a Free African Society. Eventually, he would build a new church.

> "I soon saw a large field open in seeking and instructing my African brethren, who had been a long forgotten people and few of them attended public worship."
> —John Marrant

Trouble at St. George's Church

African American membership at St. George's was growing. Many people flocked to hear Allen during an early morning Sunday service. Many of these same members attended the regular church service later in the day.

The elders felt that too many African Americans were attending the main service. New rules were made, and Allen and his friends were instructed to sit along the walls.

One day, when Allen arrived at the regular church service, he was told he could no longer sit on the main floor. All black members of the church were directed to go up the stairs and sit in the newly built gallery.

Allen and his friends walked up the stairs and took their new seats. Prayer was started. As Allen was kneeling to pray, he suddenly heard a noise. Looking up from his prayer, he saw his friend Absalom Jones praying nearby on his knees. One of the church trustees was pulling on his arm. Allen writes in his autobiography about what happened next:

> "You must not kneel here," the trustee said. He pointed to the seats around the wall.
>
> Absalom Jones replied, "Wait until prayer is over."
>
> "No," the trustee insisted. "You must get up now."
>
> Absalom Jones answered, "Wait until prayer is over, and I will get up and trouble you no more."

Not satisfied, the trustee beckoned for another trustee to help. This time they tried to pull Allen's other friend, William White, up from his knees.

By now, the prayer had ended.

With one accord, every single African American stood up with dignity and walked together out of the building.

They never looked back.

A New Purpose

It's hard for us to grasp today how monumental this action was for Richard Allen and his friends to take. In the entire history of America, this had never happened before. Many, including Richard Allen and Absalom Jones, were former slaves. Yet their self-worth and sense of justice burned so deeply within them, they dared to tell the world that racial discrimination was something they would not tolerate.

Richard Allen was determined to build a church. He persuaded three of his close friends, Absalom Jones, William White, and Dorus Ginnings, to join his passionate cause. As the spiritual leader for Philadelphia's African American community, he knew blacks needed a place to worship without racism.

He established prayer meetings. The elders at St. George forbade such gatherings. Allen and his friends rented a storeroom to hold their own services. The elders at St. George said they would erase their names from the Methodist Episcopal church membership. But Allen's campaign to build a Methodist Episcopal church for African Americans grew stronger. He raised money through subscriptions, or donations, for the new church he planned to establish.

The First Building Block

Allen also decided to form a self-help society called the Free African Society. He met with Absalom Jones to establish the rules. Together, they wrote the preamble for the society.

> *"It was proposed, after a serious communication of sentiments, that a society should be formed without regard to religious tenets."*
> —Preamble to the
> Free African Society

What a meeting that must have been! Richard Allen was 27. He was passionate about his beliefs and firm in his decisions. Forty-one-year-old Absalom Jones was much older. He was steady, yet flexible. On April 12, 1787, the two friends wrote down the guidelines for the Free African Society.

Paint a Historic Picture

When Richard Allen and Absalom Jones met to write the preamble for the Free African Society, it was a very important historic event. To commemorate this event, paint a picture that shows the two men writing this document.

Materials

★ Friends and props to use as models

★ Digital camera

★ Paints

★ Paintbrush

★ Paper suitable for painting

Before you begin to paint, try to imagine how Richard Allen and Absalom Jones sat together to write the preamble for the Free African Society. Do you think they sat at a small table? Or across from each other at a large table? Ask two of your friends to pose as models. Ask them to hold pencils and pretend to write on a piece of paper. Take pictures of your models.

What do you think Allen and Jones had on their table as they met to make their important decisions? They used quill pens and inkwells. They had parchment paper. They might even have had food or something to drink. Look on the Internet for pictures of quill pens and inkwells. Also look at actual portraits of Richard Allen (page 74) and Absalom Jones (page 93).

When you feel you have enough ideas and pictures to use for reference, you can paint your historic picture.

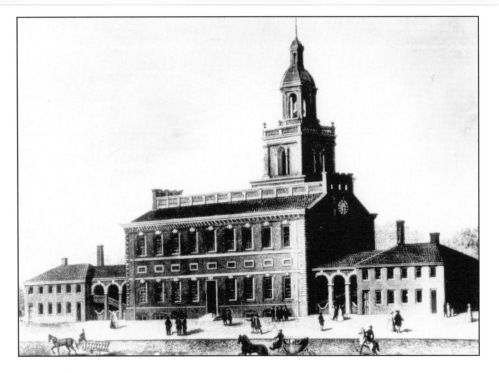

Independence Hall
Courtesy National Archives (66-G-1E-6)

On May 17, not far from Independence Hall, Richard Allen opened his home in Philadelphia for the very first meeting of the Free African Society. What thoughts must have filled his mind and those of the men who gathered with him? They knew of the delegates who were arriving in their city. They were aware of the important decisions that were soon to be made.

Richard Allen was not someone to sit idly by and wait for his future to be decided. He determined to take a stand. One week before the Constitutional Convention began, Allen officially started the very first organization for blacks, run by blacks, in the entire history of America.

The Constitutional Convention

While Allen and Jones were drafting the preamble for the Free African Society, all eyes in the newly forming nation were turning toward the city of Philadelphia. Preparations for the Constitutional Convention were underway. Independence Hall, at that time known as the State House, was opened to welcome delegates from the 13 states. Colonial leaders began arriving by ship, carriage, and horseback.

The Constitutional Convention was scheduled to start on May 14, 1787. Not enough delegates had arrived, however, so the meeting didn't begin until May 25.

> *"This characteristic quality of independent thought and action is the foundation for the greatness of Richard Allen."*
> —Charles H. Wesley

The Free African Society

So it was on May 17, 1787, the articles of association were adopted for the Free African Society. The eight men who met that day were Absalom Jones, Richard Allen, Samuel Batson, Joseph Johnson, Cato Freeman, Caesar Cranchell, James Potter, and William White.

Each member paid his dues. This money helped those in financial need. Widows and orphans of deceased members would be under the society's care.

Upright and moral behavior was required of each member. No drunkenness or disorderly actions would be tolerated. Members who did not pay their dues would be dismissed.

The amazing thing about the Free African Society is that it was the first of its kind. A precedent was established in the newly formed nation. The Free African Society announced to America that its black citizens could think for themselves, band together for support, and better their community.

Soon, the members of the Free African Society in Philadelphia contacted groups of free blacks in other communities. African societies formed in other major cities as well. Prince Hall led the Boston African Society. Newport, Rhode Island, soon had its own African Society. New York had one as well. Even as far south as Charleston, South Carolina, the Brown Fellowship Society was formed.

Drafting the Constitution

From May and all through the long, hot summer of 1787, the Constitutional Convention met at Independence Hall. Finally, in September 1787, the Constitution was drafted. The delegates signed the document and left Philadelphia. Now, each state had to approve the Constitution.

Upon reading the new Constitution, many people reacted with mixed emotions. Slavery had been an important issue. During the convention, delegates from the southern states argued that every slave should be counted when determining the representation in the House of Representatives, even though slaves would be denied the power to vote. Delegates from the northern states recognized that that plan would allow many slaveholders to be voted into office and vote for laws that supported slavery. Delegates from the northern states therefore argued that no slaves should be counted when determining the number of people a state could send to Congress.

The result of this argument and similar ones was called the Three-Fifths Compromise. Because of this compromise, the Constitution was written to state that only three out of every five slaves could be counted for representation. To Richard Allen and those who supported the abolition, or end, of slavery, this was probably a welcome decision. The Three-Fifths Compromise limited the number of slaveholders who could be elected to the House of Representatives.

However, at the Constitutional Convention, a decision had been reached about the trans-Atlantic slave trade. Congress was not allowed to make any rules about limiting the slave trade until 1808.

This was a huge disappointment. Many northern states were gradually outlawing slavery. This new rule meant that slavery could

Free African Society historic marker.
Courtesy of Mother Bethel AME Church

～ Celebrate ～
Constitution Day

On September 17, 1787, the Constitution was signed. People still celebrate this historic day today. You can join in the fun. Here are ideas to help get you started.

★ Decorate in red, white, and blue

★ Distribute small flags

★ Organize a parade

★ Sing patriotic songs

★ Wear colonial outfits

★ Serve your favorite all-American food

★ Invite everyone to sign a poster labeled "We the People!"

For more ideas on how to celebrate Constitution Day, visit the Web site http://constitutioncenter.org/ConstitutionDay/

continue to grow throughout the South, even as it was being eradicated in the north.

For the Black Founders, this was grave news indeed. Leaders of free black communities emerging throughout the nation, many of them former slaves themselves, determined anew to dedicate their lives to fighting for freedom and equality for all.

They did not fight alone. For years, the Quakers had supported the abolitionist cause. Prominent colonial leaders such as Dr. Benjamin Rush and Benjamin Franklin joined the fight. Abolitionists, both black and white, worked together during the founding years of our nation.

The Nation's New Capital

In 1790, the nation's capital was moved from New York City to Philadelphia. It would remain here for 10 years while a new capital was being built.

President George Washington arrived in Philadelphia in 1790. He moved into the President's House next to Independence Hall. Among his other servants, he brought his famous and renowned cook, Hercules, as well as Martha Washington's personal attendant, Oney Judge. Recently, archaeological work uncovered the remains of the slave quarters of the President's House in Philadelphia. Plans were started to construct a memorial.

Here in Philadelphia, the gradual emancipation law had already been passed outlawing slavery within the borders of Pennsylvania. This law stated that any slave brought into Philadelphia would gain his freedom after six months.

Washington's slaves were not set free as the laws required. Both Hercules and Oney Judge took freedom into their own hands, however, and each one escaped.

A Deep Responsibility

Richard Allen and the leaders of the free black community in Philadelphia were aware of their unique position in the newly forming nation. For 10 years important decisions about the nation would be made at Independence Hall, just down the street from Richard Allen's and the other leaders' homes. Philadelphia continued to grow and become home to the nation's largest population of free blacks.

Richard Allen believed in equality of rights. He felt it was time to establish equal rights in church. He knew it would have to

Richard Allen (1760–1831)

Richard Allen had the heart, fire, and determination of a great leader. When invited to preach in Philadelphia, he found countless free blacks throughout the city without education, religion, or jobs. He made it his personal goal to meet this need. He organized societies. He built a church. He founded a denomination. He led the fight against slavery. He stood up for equal rights. He started the National Convention Movement. Richard Allen didn't let anyone stop him on his quest to change the world. A forerunner of the modern civil rights movement, this Black Founder was the Dr. Martin Luther King Jr. of his day.

Courtesy of the Library Company of Philadelphia

$$\mathcal{B}enjamin\ \mathcal{B}anneker$$

$$(also\ known\ as\ \mathcal{B}annaker)$$

$$(1731\text{--}1806)$$

Largely self-taught, Benjamin Banneker was a genius. An amazing mathematician, he worked out intricate calculations to build the first wooden clock in America. He was also a scientist. He studied borrowed textbooks and became an avid astronomer. When a mathematician was needed to use intricate instruments and astronomical calculations to help survey the land for the nation's capital at Washington, D.C., Banneker was appointed for the job. He became famous both in the United States and England for the almanacs he wrote and published. Strongly opposed to slavery, he corresponded with Thomas Jefferson about the importance of equal rights.

Courtesy of the Maryland Historical Society

start in Philadelphia, the center of the nation. It would spread outward from there, just as had happened with the establishment of the Free African Societies. Being the brave man and free thinker that he was, he moved forward with purpose.

A Self-Taught Genius

George Washington appointed a team of men to survey the nation's new capital. At that time, the commissioners named the capital city Washington after the first president. The commissioners also named the total area set aside to include the new city as the District of Columbia in honor of Christopher Columbus.

One of the members of the surveying team was a mathematical genius and self-taught astronomer, Benjamin Banneker. Banneker was well known in his neighborhood. His ancestors had settled near Baltimore, Maryland. His grandmother, Molly Welsh, was English. As a young orphan, she lived in England and worked as a milkmaid. One day, young Molly was milking a cow when the cow kicked over the bucket of milk. The farmer accused Banneker's grandmother of stealing the milk. Molly was banished from England and sent to America as an indentured servant. She eventually received her freedom.

Molly Welsh purchased land in Maryland and a couple of slaves to help her farm. Eventually, she freed the slaves. By then, she had fallen in love with one, Bannka, a prince from Africa. They married and had a daughter named Mary. Mary grew up, married a freed slave, and together they had four children. Benjamin was the oldest. By then, the name of Bannka had changed to Banneker.

Benjamin Banneker was a bright lad. His grandmother Molly taught him to read from the family Bible. Benjamin worked hard to help his family on their tobacco farm. When a Quaker opened an integrated school, Benjamin was eager to attend.

Schooling was all too short, however. His father died when he was young, and the family needed him to farm. He continued his studies on his own. Borrowing every textbook he could, Benjamin studied a wide variety of subjects. Mathematics was one of his favorites.

Famous Inventor and Amazing Astronomer

Benjamin Banneker decided to make a clock. Using precise mathematical calculations, he drew the many intricate parts for the clock. He then whittled each piece out of wood. When the clock was finished, it worked perfectly.

Neighbors came from far and wide to see his amazing clock. He became known as a famous inventor. His clock was the first one ever made entirely in America, and it kept perfect time as long as he lived.

As he grew older, his interests expanded. When his good friend George Ellicott took up astronomy, Banneker became fascinated with the stars as well. Night after night, he could be seen leaving his log cabin carrying a telescope and a warm blanket. Wrapping up in the blanket, he'd stay out most of the night, looking up at the stars. He noted their paths across the night sky and calculated mathematical observations. He used his complex calculations to make important scientific predictions such as when a solar eclipse would occur.

Building the Nation's New Capital

When President George Washington appointed a team to survey the new capital, they needed a mathematician. Pierre L'Enfant was commissioned to oversee the project and draw the maps. Andrew Ellicott, the cousin of Benjamin Banneker's friend George, was appointed as surveyor. He asked Benjamin Banneker to be part of the team.

Banneker set up his telescope inside a tent and pointed it out through a hole up toward the night sky. He observed the paths the stars took through the sky. He kept careful records and wrote down complex mathematical calculations. These numbers were then used to determine the precise layout of the streets.

Map a Capital City

Materials

★ Pencil

★ Graph paper

★ Drawing paper

Benjamin Banneker was part of a team to survey and map the new capital of the United States. Just imagine that you were appointed to help map a brand new capital city. What kind of layout for the streets would you design? Which government buildings would you plan for?

To give you ideas, look at street maps of capital cities in different countries. Use an atlas, or visit Google Earth on the Internet.

To make it easier to draw a map, pencil in your initial ideas on graph paper. When you're satisfied with the design, transfer it to a larger piece of paper. After it's done, give your new capital city a name!

A disagreement between the leaders of the project and L'Enfant occurred, and L'Enfant was dismissed. Enraged, L'Enfant took his detailed maps with him. All their hard work might have been wasted, but Banneker had kept careful records of all of his calculations. He was able to work with the surveying team to draw up new maps. The nation's new capital was built as it had originally been planned.

Benjamin Banneker's Almanacs

After surveying, Benjamin Banneker turned his attention to a project he'd been thinking about for a long time. He decided to write and publish an almanac.

In those days, an almanac was a very important book. Farmers read an almanac to know when to plant which crops. Sailors read an almanac to find out when the tides rose and fell. Homemakers read an almanac looking for delicious recipes. Everyone read an almanac for entertainment, jokes, mathematical puzzles, and fascinating trivia.

Writing an almanac was a tremendous undertaking. Most almanac writers, including Benjamin Franklin, used information and calculations for star charts and seasons based on documents published in England. Banneker decided to use all his own calculations.

In 1792, he published his very first almanac: *Benjamin Banneker's Pennsylvania,*

Delaware, Maryland and Virginia Almanack and Ephemeris, for the Year of Our Lord, 1792. It was an instant success and launched him into international fame.

Letters to Thomas Jefferson

Benjamin Banneker sent a copy of his almanac to the secretary of state, Thomas Jefferson. Along with it, he wrote a letter voicing his strong opinion against slavery. Amazed and delighted at the genius of the man behind this marvelous publication, Thomas Jefferson wrote a reply. Both letters were eventually published. These letters, and the almanacs Banneker wrote, were supported widely by abolitionists. Many copies of his almanacs sold both in the United States and in England. Banneker continued to write and publish a new almanac each year for the next five years.

> *"I am of the African race, and in the color which is natural to them of the deepest dye; and it under a sense of the most profound gratitude to the Supreme Being of the universe."*
>
> —Benjamin Banneker

Write a Government Official

Benjamin Banneker wrote a letter to Thomas Jefferson. His letter can still be read today. Just like Banneker did, you can write a letter to a government official—you can even write to the president. To help you find the name and contact information of your representatives and government officials, check out the following Web sites:

The White House: www.whitehouse.gov/CONTACT/ Your Representative: https://writerep.house.gov/writerep/welcome.shtml

Here are several tips to help you write your letter:

1. One page works best. Government officials are very busy people. Keep your letter short, and it will be easier to read.

2. Use your letter to express your opinion about one single topic in a polite and clear way.

3. Be sure to thank your government official for reading your letter.

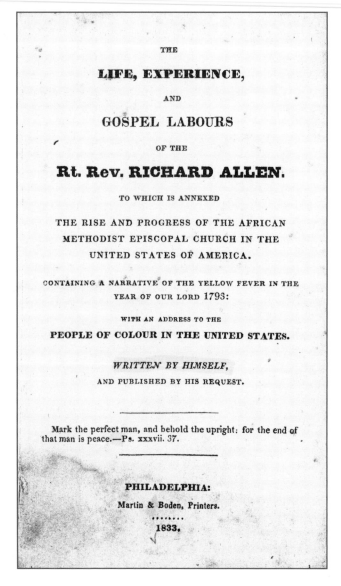

Richard Allen published a firsthand account of the Yellow Fever Epidemic of 1793 along with his autobiography *The Life, Experience and Gospel Labours of the Rt. Rev. Richard Allen.*

Used with Permission of Documenting the American South, the University of North Carolina at Chapel Hill Libraries

The Yellow Fever Epidemic of 1793

In the late summer of 1793, however, a terrible epidemic of yellow fever swept through the city of Philadelphia. Panic gripped the city. Those with money headed out to the countryside. Nobody knew that the terrible fever was actually spread by bites from mosquitoes that carried the disease.

Richard Allen and Absalom Jones met together and discussed the devastating epidemic. Allen and Jones, along with their friend William Gray, decided to step forward and organize assistance.

They visited the mayor of Philadelphia to offer their help. The mayor was relieved and thankful at this tremendous demonstration of humanitarianism. Jones and Gray took charge of visiting the sick, while Allen oversaw the burial of the dead. Dr. Benjamin Rush, the city's leading physician during this epidemic, taught Jones, Allen, and their helpers how to provide advanced medical treatment. Allen and Jones organized their efforts and immediately went throughout the city.

What they found was appalling. Sick people were left alone. Dead bodies were everywhere. All throughout the city, everyone was so afraid of the disease that as soon as someone became sick, no one would help that person for fear of catching the fever themselves.

They did not understand that yellow fever was spread through the bites of mosquitoes.

Richard Allen, Absalom Jones, and their helpers did whatever they could. Following the doctor's instructions, they provided the best medical care of the day to over 800 people, many of whom got better because of their efforts. They stayed with people who were sick and abandoned by their family. They buried the dead. When they entered homes and found children all alone because both parents had died, they tenderly took them to the orphans' house.

Over 300 members of Philadelphia's black community died, many of them getting the disease while assisting others. It was a time filled with terror and dread, yet even though they could have left the city for the safety of the countryside, Richard Allen, Absalom Jones, and many other free blacks stayed behind and helped.

Fall finally came. The cold temperatures killed the mosquito population. The epidemic came to an end. Over 5,000 of Philadelphia's citizens had died.

Freedom to Worship

Once that terrible epidemic was over, Richard Allen, Absalom Jones, and their friends turned their attention back to building a church. Money was needed, so they raised funds. Leaders such as Benjamin Rush gave

Organize a Helpful Event

Print out a list of community service ideas from the Web site of 366 Community Service Ideas at http://lancaster.unl.edu/4h/serviceideas.shtml. Next, grab your friends, study the list, discuss opportunities that interest all of you, and vote on a project to do together to help people in your community.

generously. The very first day that Allen and Jones went out to collect donations, they collected $360—even George Washington was said to have made a donation.

A vacant lot was found. During the ground-breaking ceremony, Richard Allen, himself, dug the first shovel of dirt. As plans for building the church continued, an election was held. The majority voted to establish this church as belonging to the Church of England. Only Richard Allen and Absalom Jones voted to have a Methodist Church.

It was easy to understand why so many voted for the Church of England. The leaders of St. George's Methodist Episcopal Church had continued to harass and threaten the building of an African American church each step of the way. Yet Allen still believed strongly in building a Methodist Episcopal Church. The Methodists were the first organization to bring Christianity to those who were enslaved. The Methodists taught about the equality of each person's soul, both black and white. Allen would be a staunch Methodist until the day he died.

By now, he had a substantial number of fellow black Methodists who also supported his plans. Allen and his friends purchased a building that was formerly used as a blacksmith shop. Allen had the blacksmith shop hauled to a vacant lot he had purchased on Sixth near Lombard Street. Hiring carpenters to repair the wooden frame, he, himself, built the pulpit.

That is how Philadelphia soon became home to two churches for African Americans.

(above) Richard Allen's pulpit.
Courtesy of Mother Bethel AME Church

(right) Engraving showing the blacksmith shop Richard Allen purchased being hauled to its new location as the Bethel African Methodist Episcopal Church.
The Historical Society of Pennsylvania (HSP), "Goal, in Walnut Street Philadelphia," engraving by William Birch, c. 1794, Society Print Collection (Bd531.2)

(far right) Mother Bethel AME Church historic marker.
Courtesy of Mother Bethel AME Church

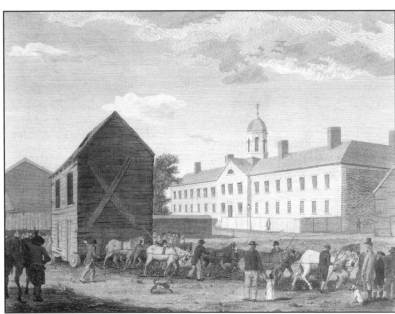

MOTHER BETHEL
A.M.E. CHURCH
Founded on ground purchased by Richard Allen in 1787, this congregation is the mother church of the African Methodist Episcopal denomination. The present structure, erected 1889, replaces three earlier churches on this site.
PENNSYLVANIA HISTORICAL AND MUSEUM COMMISSION 1991

On July 17, 1794, the African Church in Philadelphia, at first part of the Church of England before becoming the African Episcopal Church of St. Thomas, held its first service. Reverend Absalom Jones was established as its minister.

And on July 29, 1794, Bethel African Methodist Episcopal (AME) Church, eventually to become known as Mother Bethel AME Church, was dedicated. Reverend Richard Allen invited a guest minister to preach as well as a second guest minister to sing hymns and pray the prayer of dedication.

A Thriving City

Other leaders stepped forward in Philadelphia. The first African Presbyterian Church and the first African Baptist Church were established. New societies were formed—literary societies, moral societies, musical societies, and abolitionist societies. Schools for children of free blacks were opened.

Philadelphia's community of free blacks also worked diligently to establish a steady livelihood and solid home life. Among other jobs, Richard Allen was a chimney sweep and a shoemaker. Cyrus Bustill, head of a family that would become famous as abolitionists, was a prosperous baker. James Forten, who owned a sailmaking loft, became one of Philadelphia's wealthiest merchants. Some women took in laundry. Vendors could be heard on

Absalom Jones (1746-1818)

As one of the nation's most influential Black Founders, Absalom Jones helped lead the way to social, moral, educational, and religious freedoms for African Americans. He cofounded the Free African Society and he helped found the African Episcopal Church of St. Thomas in Philadelphia. He was ordained the first black Episcopal priest and served faithfully at St. Thomas's for over 20 years. A close friend of Richard Allen his entire life, Jones helped organize aid for the nation's capital during the Yellow Fever Epidemic of 1793. Together with Allen and James Forten, he helped organize protection for Philadelphia during the War of 1812. Pursuing his personal education with passion, working tirelessly to purchase the freedom of both his wife and himself, Absalom Jones rose up to organize and help lead the new nation's largest community of free blacks.

Used with Permission of Documenting the American South, the University of North Carolina at Chapel Hill Libraries

Wood-sawyer

Laundress

Rag-picker

Whitewasher

the streets calling out to customers. Pepper pot soup, a favorite in this city since the days of Valley Forge, was sold on the street corners. "Pepper pot! Smoking hot!" women cried to passersby. Wherever work or jobs were available within the busy nation's capital, men and women of Philadelphia's community of free blacks could be found hard at work.

Philadelphia's Wealthy Sailmaker

James Forten owned a sailmaking loft in Philadelphia. One of the city's wealthiest and prosperous merchants, he became close friends with Richard Allen and Absalom Jones. These three Black Founders led the free black community in Philadelphia. Together, they reached out to free black communities all across the newly forming nation. Together, their pamphlets of protests, petitions, religious organizations, and societies worked as one force to influence the nation.

James Forten's great-grandfather had first arrived in Philadelphia on a slave ship a year or two after William Penn. James Forten's father, freeborn in Philadelphia, became a sailmaker. As a youth, James attended the African School in Philadelphia. Part of one of Philadelphia's oldest families, James Forten grew up to spend the rest of his life as an active citizen of the city.

The port of Philadelphia, 1768.
Courtesy National Archives (208-LU-25F-14)

Forten employed both whites and blacks at his loft, as well as his own sons. His loft supplied sails for the many ships that sailed in and out of Philadelphia's busy port. He did not allow any drinking or misconduct by his workers, but expected them to be moral and upright men. This was a striking difference from the typical workers found at the docks. Many sailors and dockworkers were known as troublesome. This was not true of the men who worked at Forten's sail loft. He saw to it that his workers lived honest and good lives.

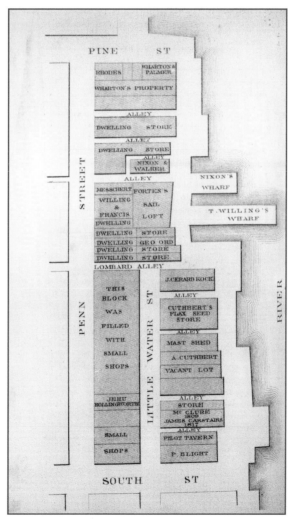

(left) Map of businesses showing James Forten's sail loft.
Courtesy of the Library Company of Philadelphia

(above) Dock along the river's edge in Philadelphia.
Photo by author

(top) James Forten's home.

(bottom) James Forten's historic marker.

Photos by author

JAMES FORTEN
(1766 - 1842)

A wealthy sailmaker who employed multi-racial craftsmen, Forten was a leader of the African-American community in Philadelphia and a champion of reform causes. The American Antislavery Society was organized in his house here in 1833.

PENNSYLVANIA HISTORICAL AND MUSEUM COMMISSION 1990

James Forten (1766–1842)

As a young lad, James Forten served bravely aboard a privateer during the American Revolution. When he returned home, he was apprenticed to work in a sailmaking loft. Forten eventually became owner of the loft and amassed a great fortune.

Inventor, businessman, abolitionist, and community leader, Forten was one of the most respected citizens of Philadelphia. His letters and articles of protest appeared frequently in newspapers. Outspoken against the American Colonization Society, his influence caused many people to join the fight against the society's efforts to relocate free blacks in Liberia, Africa.

Forten married Charlotte Vandine after his first wife died. They had eight children. They often opened their home to people in need. The Forten household became a hub of abolitionist activity and a center for political activism. Their daughters and sons grew up to become frequent speakers and prolific writers in the fight against slavery, along with their spouses. The Forten grandchildren also became well-known abolitionists. During the Civil War, the Fortens' granddaughter Charlotte Forten Grimké was a teacher to newly freed slaves on the South Carolina Sea Islands. After serving as an assistant surgeon in the army during the Civil War, the Fortens' grandson Charles Burleigh Purvis became the first African American to oversee a hospital with his appointment at the Freedman's Hospital in Washington, D.C.

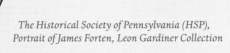

*The Historical Society of Pennsylvania (HSP),
Portrait of James Forten, Leon Gardiner Collection*

Charlotte Vandine Forten
(1785–1884)

A founding member of the Philadelphia Female Anti-Slavery Society, Charlotte Forten opened her home to leading black and white abolitionists. Wife of prosperous businessman and sailmaker James Forten, Charlotte Forten was also a shrewd business-woman who invested in real estate. She and her husband raised eight children to become outstanding citizens and leaders of the Philadelphia community of free blacks. Both she and her daughters were active founding members of the Philadelphia Female Anti-Slavery Society. Her home was a frequent stop on the Underground Railroad. She welcomed fugitive slaves, hid them in secret hideaways, and helped them along their journey.

Courtesy Francis Grimké Papers,
Moorland-Spingarn Research Center,
Howard University

James Forten's sail loft manufactured and supplied sails for ships landing at the busy port of Philadelphia.

Photo by author

Philadelphia's African Lodge

Many Founding Fathers joined as members of Freemasonry. George Washington was a Mason. Benjamin Franklin was a Mason. Philadelphia's Black Founders joined the ranks as well. In 1797, Richard Allen, Absalom Jones, and James Forten communicated with Prince Hall about the need for Philadelphia to have a lodge of black Masons.

On September 22, 1797, Prince Hall traveled from Boston to Philadelphia. He officiated over the installation of officers for Philadelphia's new lodge. Absalom Jones was installed as the Worshipful Master, or leader of the lodge. Richard Allen was installed as the Treasurer. James Forten also devoted a great deal of time to the lodge.

Members of Philadelphia's African Lodge took their roles very seriously. Caring for widows and orphans, committed to living moral lives, and passionate about the pursuit of education, the Masons of the African Lodge in Philadelphia dedicated their lives to making an important difference in their world.

One of the most important dates on the Masonic calendar was the Feast of St. John the Baptist. When the Masons held a parade in 1797 to celebrate the holiday in the nation's capital, Absalom Jones and his fellow members marched along. When a parade was held to honor President George Washington after he had passed away, the African Lodge of Philadelphia once more marched.

Officiating over Philadelphia's African Lodge, Prince Hall helped form lodges in other cities as well. Hall provided charters and became the Provincial Grand Master over these new lodges. His speeches, pamphlets, and encouraging visits helped pave the way.

Protests and Petitions

In 1793, a detestable law was passed called the Fugitive Slave Act. This law stated that fugitives, or escaping slaves, could be legally arrested and returned to their masters. This law stated that magistrates in each city had the power to enforce this law, and that anyone helping a fugitive slave could be fined.

This law was a devastating blow to slaves and abolitionists. Not only did it endanger the fragile freedoms of runaways, it also endangered the welfare of anyone who helped them.

Richard Allen, Absalom Jones, and James Forten, along with Philadelphia's community of free blacks, took a stand. Many of them lived within walking distance of Independence Hall, where Congress met and the President of the United States presided. They knew they held an important position in the community and had a unique influence over what decisions were made. They protested through letters, sermons, newspaper articles, and pamphlets. Time after time, they sent petitions to Independence Hall, addressed to Congress and the president, declaring the need for justice and liberty to prevail.

Freedom! Freedom for All!

The year was 1799. It was the last year the nation's capital would be in the city of Philadelphia. Thomas Jefferson was now president. And the Black Founders of Philadelphia were hard at work.

A petition was written. Its passionate cry to bring an end to the horrible Atlantic slave trade still rings across the centuries. The appeal for justice to outweigh the detested Fugitive Slave Act still stirs the hearts of all who read it. The eloquent testimony of the rights of all humankind still shines bright and clear. Absalom Jones and 73 other members of Philadelphia's free black community, including Richard Allen, signed this petition on December 30, 1799.

The petition was very influential. Its heartfelt cry was a loud voice in the antislavery cause. Abolitionists, both black and white, were strengthened to continue the fight. Government leaders were weighing slavery in the balance. The Constitution stated that in 1808, Congress would be allowed to make a decision either to continue the trans-Atlantic slave trade or stop it.

This petition from Philadelphia's free blacks, and others like it, were monumental instruments placed inside the room where Congress met. Even though the doors of Independence Hall were closed to African Americans, their voices still were heard within its walls. Passionate, eloquent, and educated Black Founders let their concerns be known to the nation's new government through the petitions they wrote and submitted.

Here is the petition of December 30, 1799, in its entirety.

Petition of Absalom Jones and Seventy-Three Others
To the President, Senate, and House of Representatives.

The Petition of the People of Colour, free men, within the City and Suburbs of Philadelphia, humbly showeth,

That, thankful to God, our Creator, and to the Government under which we live, for the blessings and benefits granted to us in the enjoyment of our natural right to liberty, and the protection of our persons and property from the oppression and violence which so great a number of like colour and national descent are subject to, we feel ourselves bound, from a sense of these blessings, to continue in our respective allotments, and to lead honest and peaceable lives, rendering due submission unto the laws, and exciting and encouraging each other thereto, agreeable to the uniform advice of our friends of every denomination; yet while we feel impressed with grateful sensations for the Providential favour we ourselves enjoy, we cannot be insensible of the condition of our afflicted brethren, suffering under various circumstances, in different parts of these states; but deeply sympathizing with them, are incited by a sense of social duty, and humbly conceive ourselves authorized to address and petition you on their behalf, believing them to be objects of your representation in your public councils, in common with ourselves and every other class of citizens within the jurisdiction of the United States, according to the design (cont'd next page) of the present Constitution, formed by the General Convention, and ratified in the different states, as set forth in the preamble thereto in the following words, viz. "We, the people of the United States, in order to form a more perfect union, establish justice, insure domestic tranquility, provide for the common defence, and to secure the blessings of liberty to ourselves and posterity, do ordain, &c." We apprehend this solemn compact is violated, by a trade carried on in a clandestine manner, to the coast of Guinea, and another equally wicked, practiced openly by citizens of some of the southern states, upon the waters of Maryland and Delaware; men sufficiently callous to qualify them for the brutal purpose, are employed in kidnapping those of our brethren that are free, and purchasing others of such as claim a property in them: thus, those poor helpless victims, like droves of cattle, are seized, fettered, and hurried into places provided for this most horrid traffic, such as dark cellars and garrets, as is notorious at Northwestfork, Chestertown, Eastown, and divers other places. After a sufficient number is obtained, they are forced on board vessels, crowded under hatches, without the least commiseration, left to deplore the sad separation of the dearest ties in nature, husband from wife, and parents from children; thus packed together, they are transported to Georgia and other places, and there inhumanely exposed to sale. Can any commerce, trade, or transaction so detestably shock the feeling of man, or degrade the dignity of his nature equal to this? And how increasingly is the evil aggravated, when practiced in a land high in profession of the benign doctrines of our Blessed Lord, who taught his followers to do unto others as they would they should do unto them. Your petitioners desire not to enlarge, though volumes might be filled with the sufferings of this grossly abused part of the human species, seven hundred thousand of whom, it is said, are not in unconditional bondage in these states: but conscious of the rectitude of our motives in a concern so nearly affecting us, and so effectually interesting to the welfare of this country, we cannot but address you as

guardians of our rights, and patrons of equal and national liberties, hoping you will view the subject in an impartial, unprejudiced light. We do not ask for an immediate emancipation of all, knowing that the degraded state of many, and their want of education, would greatly disqualify for such a change; yet, humble desire you may exert every means in your power to undo the heavy burdens, and prepare the way for the oppressed to go free, that every yoke may be broken. The law not long since enacted by Congress, called the Fugitive Bill, is in its execution found to be attended with circumstances peculiarly hard and distressing; for many of our afflicted brethren, in order to avoid the barbarities wantonly exercised upon them, or through fear of being carried off by those men-stealers, being forced to seek refuge by flight, they are then, by armed men, under colour of this law, cruelly treated, or brought back in chains to those that have no claim upon them. In the Constitution and the Fugitive Bill, no mention is made of black people, or slaves; therefore, if the Bill of Rights, or the Declaration of congress are of any validity, we beseech, that as we are men, we may be admitted to partake of the liberties and unalienable rights therein held forth; firmly believing that the extending of justice and equity to all classes would be a means of drawing down the blessing of Heaven upon this land, for the peace and prosperity of which, and the real happiness of every member of the community, we fervently pray.

Philadelphia, 30th of December, 1799

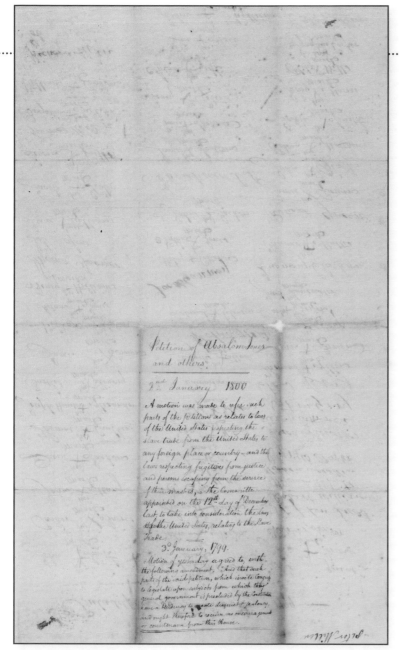

Petition of Absalom Jones, Richard Allen, and others.

Courtesy National Archives (HR 6A-F4.2, RG 233)

Chester-town, Eas-town, and divers other places;— After a sufficient number is obtained, they are forced on board vessels, crouded under hatches, and without the least commiseration, left to deplore the sad separation of the dearest ties in nature, husband from wife and Parents from children, thus pack'd together they are transported to Georgia and other places, and there inhumanly exposed to sale: Can any Commerce, trade, or transaction, so detestably shock the feelings of Men, or degrade the dignity of his nature equal to this, and how increasingly is the evil aggravated when practised in a Land, high in profession of the benign doctrines of our blessed Lord, who taught his followers to do unto others as they would they should do unto them?

Your petitioners desire not to enlarge, tho volumes might be filled with the sufferings of this grossly abused class of the human species, (700.000 of whom it is said are now in unconditional bondage in these States,) but, conscious of the rectitude of our motives in a concern so nearly affecting us, and so essentially interesting to real welfare of this Country, we cannot but address you as Guardians of our Civil rights, and Patrons of equal and National Liberty, hoping you will view the subject in an impartial, unprejudiced manner. We do not ask for the immediate eman-cipation of all, knowing that the degraded state of many, and their want of education, would greatly disqualify for such a change; yet humbly desire you may exert every means in your power to undo the heavy burdens, and prepare the way for the oppressed to go free, that every yoke may be broken.

The Law not long since enacted by Congress called the Fugitive Bill is, in its execution found to be attended with circumstances peculiarly hard and distressing, for many of our afflicted Brethren in order to avoid the barbarities wantonly exercised upon them, or thro fear of being carried off by those Men-stealers, have been forced to seek refuge by flight; they are then hunted by armed Men, and under colour of this law, cruelly treated, shot, or brought back in chains to those who have no just claim upon them.

In the Constitution, and the Fugitive bill, no mention is made of Black people or Slaves—therefore if the Bill of Rights, or the declaration of Congress are of any validity, we beseech that as we are men, we may be admitted to partake of the Liberties and unalienable Rights therein held forth— firmly believing that the extending of Justice and equity to all Classes, would be a means of drawing down the blessing of Heaven upon this Land, for the Peace and Prosperity of which, and the real happiness of every member of the Community, we fervently pray—

Philadelphia 30th of December 1799—

John Smith his mark +
Asher Harris his mark
John Mang his mark
David Jackson his mark
Thomas Caulker his mark
Joseph Houston + Alexander his mark
Bartlet Tinney his mark
James Brown his mark
William Laure his mark
Adam James his mark
Henry Williams his mark
Thomas Serener
Lot Rasine
Isaac Williams his mark
Jacob Gibbs his mark
Severn Culton his mark
James Wilson
Benjamin Jackson his mark
William Coulson his mark
Richard Allen
Cob Albert his mark

Samuel Wilson his mark
John Nelson his mark
Thomas Walton his mark
Edward Matthews his mark
Anthony Williams his mark
John Harris his mark
Philip Johnson his mark
Edward Simon
Charles Caldwell his mark
Peter Glover
Ishmael Robinson his mark
Joe Conway
Wiley Cotton +
Nathan Jones his mark
John McJackson work
Abraham Dee
James Scotton his mark
Prince Lprence his mark
Henry Peters his mark
Adam Hoff his mark
John Yall his mark

Absalom Jones
John Jones his mark
Moses Johnson
St?
Robert
William
Stephen Miller
Cyrus Porter
Jacob Nicholson
Alex. Heathcoat
Nathan Gray
Chas. Harry
Thomas Allen his mark
Cesar Brown his mark
Charles Burton his mark
Riley
Jacob Lancaster mark
Quomony Clarkson
Thomas Mattis his mark
Robert Green
James Bowen his mark
John Black his mark
Peter Matthews his mark
John Smith his mark
John Morris his mark
Philip Wells his mark
Nathan Cooper his mark
Cato Collins

Write a Petition

If you want to get something important done in your school or community, a petition is the perfect way to start. First, identify your cause, or what needs to be changed. Second, clearly describe who supports your cause. Third, provide a reason explaining why your cause is important. Here is an example:

We, the students of Eucalyptus High, petition the school district to not drop drama from its list of available subjects. Studying performing arts provides students with a well-rounded education, and dramatic performances help benefit the community as a whole.

Type up your petition and add lines for people to sign their names. Number each line to make it easier to count. Make photocopies of your petition, clip each one to a clipboard, attach a pen with a piece of yarn, and send out volunteers to get signatures.

Rev. Richard Allen.

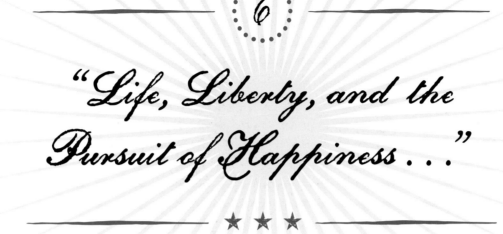

6

"Life, Liberty, and the Pursuit of Happiness..."

★ ★ ★

AFRICAN AMERICANS LEAD THE WAY

As a Black Founder, Richard Allen forged the way. Yet even though he was often the first to accomplish the many great brave and heroic deeds he became known for, he was not alone. He was surrounded by others who shared the same goals. They shared a great, common passion to see African Americans given their full rights. This passion was the glue that held Philadelphia's community of free blacks together. This passion was the glue that connected Black Founders in Philadelphia with free blacks in other cities. This passion was the glue that united all African Americans during the founding years of the new nation.

Richard Allen, Founder of the African Methodist Episcopal Church, in the United States of America, 1779.
Courtesy of the Library Company of Philadelphia

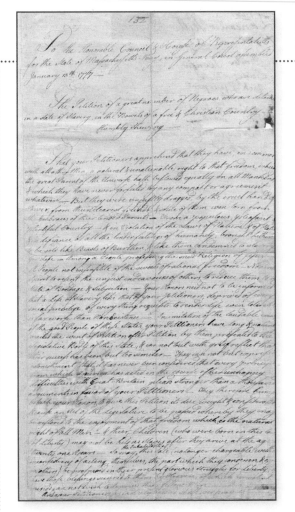

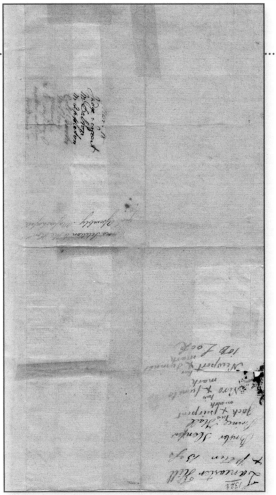

Prince Hall's petition of 1777.
Courtesy of Massachusetts Archives

Boston's Black Founders

Richard Allen, Absalom Jones, and James Forten of Philadelphia were connected with Boston's Black Founders. They communicated together, visited one another, and kept in touch. During this era, the most prominent free black of Boston was Prince Hall. Hall had established his leadership in Boston when he organized the lodge of Freemasonry in 1775. He owned and operated the leather goods shop in Boston called the Golden Fleece. His frequent speeches, numerous petitions, newspaper articles and pamphlets, and personal letters were a powerful influence.

In 1777, Prince Hall and eight other Bostonians signed a petition to the General Court of Massachusetts demanding complete abolition of slavery. In 1787, Hall and 73 other men submitted a petition to the General Court of Massachusetts detailing a "back-to-Africa" plan. Nine months later, Hall and the free blacks of Boston submitted yet another petition demanding equal education for their children.

These petitions carried a heavy weight of influence. In a time when the Massachusetts state government was considering emancipation, the voice of Hall and his fellow black citizens rang out loud and clear through their petitions. Massachusetts was one of the first states to make a pivotal decision regarding emancipation—and the influence of Prince Hall and the Black Founders of Boston was paramount.

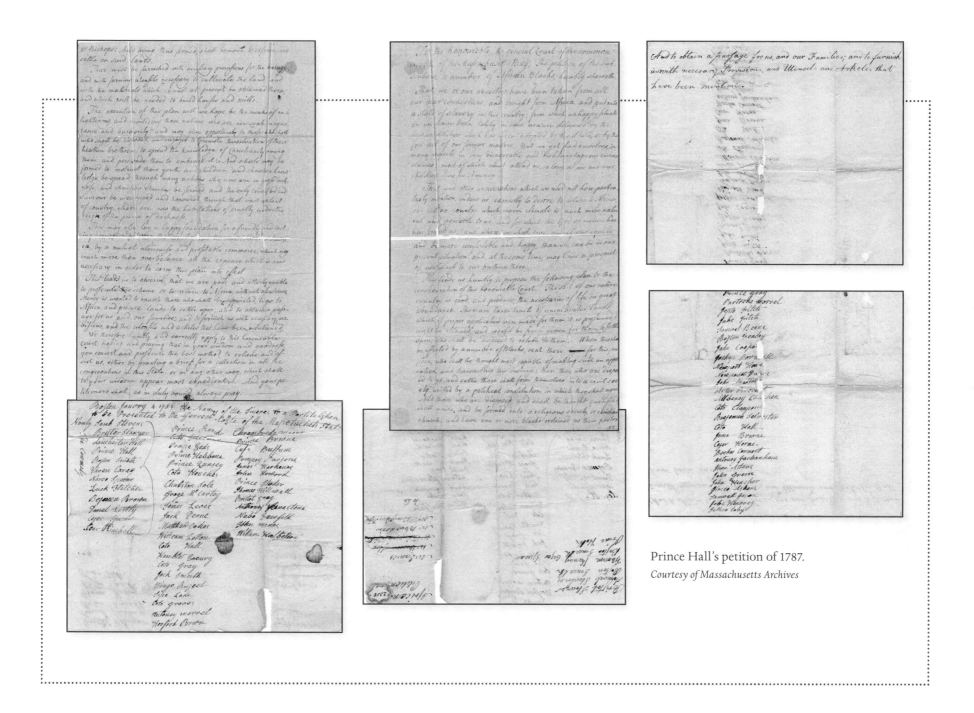

Prince Hall's petition of 1787.

Courtesy of Massachusetts Archives

Prince Hall (c. 1735–1807)

Prince Hall was big because he did things in a big way. There were no well-known organizations for free blacks to join, so Prince Hall started one. He is considered the founder of black Freemasonry. There were no civil rights leaders for African Americans, so Prince Hall became one. He organized the free blacks of Boston and led them in the fight for equal rights. There were no schools for African American children in Boston, so Prince Hall established one. He held a school in his own home with teachers from Harvard.

And biggest of all: slavery existed in America. Prince Hall fought against it. He organized and wrote petitions, gathered signatures from his friends, and sent them to the Massachusetts Legislature. Massachusetts outlawed slavery within its state in 1783. The trans-Atlantic slave trade legally came to an end in 1808. Prince Hall stands tall in the hall of people who shaped history in an important way.

Kidnapped!

In February of 1788, the community of free blacks in Boston was all astir—three of its citizens had been kidnapped and sold as slaves! These three men had been hired to work aboard a ship anchored at Boston, but the ship suddenly set sail. They were trapped on board and sold in the West Indies as slaves.

Prince Hall and the free blacks of Boston wrote a petition and submitted it to the General Court of Massachusetts. This petition had amazing results. John Hancock, the governor of Massachusetts, contacted the government in the West Indies on behalf of the kidnapped men.

The General Court voted in March to outlaw the slave trade in Massachusetts. Slave ships could no longer land at Boston and other Massachusetts ports.

Meanwhile, the three kidnapped citizens of Boston were protesting to the authorities in West Indies. The government made arrangements for them to be set free. By July, they returned home to Boston. Their family and friends were overcome with joy, and what a sense of victory Prince Hall and Boston's Black Founders must have experienced.

Joining the Fight

Some of the citizens who joined Prince Hall were Black Founders such as John Marrant and George Middleton. Marrant was ordained as the chaplain of Prince Hall's African Lodge 459. During the Festival of St. John, Marrant delivered an influential anti-slavery sermon. This sermon was published for all to read.

George Middleton, leader of the Bucks of America during the American Revolution, was a founding member of the African Society as well as other societies in Boston. A Prince Hall Mason, Middleton was initiated as its third Grand Master. He was also a strong advocate for equal education.

Cemeteries and Burial Grounds

One of the responsibilities leaders of the free black communities took upon themselves was to help with burials. Because of racism, African Americans were often not welcomed in a city or church's cemeteries. They had to find and establish burial grounds of their own. In 1790, the Free African Society in Philadelphia rented burial grounds called Potter's Fields.

George Middleton (c. ?–1810)

Hero. Patriot. Advocate. George Middleton was a natural leader. During the American Revolution, Colonel Middleton led an all-black unit in Boston called the Bucks of America. Governor John Hancock honored his leadership by presenting him with a flag bearing the unit's emblem of a buck, or deer. After the war, Middleton was a founding member and leader of anti-slavery societies and self-improvement societies in Boston. He joined the Prince Hall Masons, eventually becoming its Third Grand Master. This Black Founder also left his mark on history by petitioning the government for equal education.

Built around 1797, George Middleton's house on Pinkney Street in Boston is now part of Boston's Black Heritage Trail. It is the oldest home built by an African American in that area that is still standing.

Courtesy of John Schrantz

(counterclockwise)

Construction phase of monument for African Burial Ground, New York City.

African Burial Ground Way, New York City.

Photos by author

Completed portion of monument at African Burial Ground, New York City.

Courtesy of Joan L. Pantsios

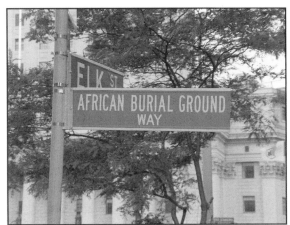

In modern times, important discoveries have been made about burial grounds. In Portsmouth, New Hampshire, the "Negro Burying Ground" was discovered. It is now part of Portsmouth's Black Heritage Trail.

In New York City, during construction in the 1990s, the African Burial Ground was discovered. Archaeologists found the remains of over 400 graves. Many skeletons were still intact. Numerous artifacts were found, such as buttons bearing the anchor and rope design of the British navy. Beads and rings were found, much of the jewelry holding significant meaning representing the African culture. To honor the lives of the men, women, and children who lived and died in America, many of them enslaved, a special ceremony was held. A memorial was built over the site.

In Newport, Rhode Island, there is a cemetery called God's Little Acre. Unlike other colonial African burial grounds, God's Little Acre is still in existence today. Tombstones can be found there dating back to the late 1600s.

Some of the tombstones were cut by Pompey Stevens. Many historians think this is the man also known as Zingo Stevens. A stonecutter and polisher by trade, the designs he cut into the tombstones are works of art. His family is buried in God's Little Acre.

Many of Newport Gardner's family members are also buried in God's Little Acre. Newport Gardner was one of Newport's leading citizens. Several of his children died while young, and their tombstones can be seen today.

Originally arriving in this busy seaport as a teenager, Newport Gardner had been born in West Africa before being kidnapped, sold into slavery, and eventually set free. Newport Gardner was an accomplished musician. He became the first African American to publish a musical composition. One of the songs attributed to him is called "Crooked Shanks."

Newport Gardner was a leader of the free black community in the city of Newport, Rhode Island. A founding member of the African Union Society, he believed in education, self-improvement, and civil rights. He helped establish a school and became the head teacher. He longed to return to his beloved Africa, the land of his birth. In his 80s, he and one of his sons joined a small group of African Americans who sailed back across the Atlantic Ocean to Africa as missionaries.

Arts and Crafts

Zingo Stevens was a stonecutter. Newport Gardner was a musician. Many African Americans during the founding years of the new nation were skilled artisans and craftsmen.

One of these artists was Dave Drake, a potter by trade. Dave was famous for his incredible talent of shaping clay into pots. Not just small, ordinary pots. Dave the potter wrestled with humongous chunks of clay to turn out gigantic ceramic jugs.

Dave is the most famous of the potters who worked in the plantation potteries in Edgefield, South Carolina. He knew how to read and write at a time when it was against the law for slaves to be educated. Dave carved verses and rhymes into the clay on the huge pots he made. He also signed many of his pots with his name. Here are some of the verses he wrote.

Put every bit all between
surely this jar will hold 14
12 July 1834

I wonder where is all my relations
Friendship to all—and every nation
16 August 1857

A very large jar which has four handles
Pack it full of fresh meat—then light candles
12 April 1858

The forth of July is surely come
To blow the fife and beat the drum.
4 July 1859

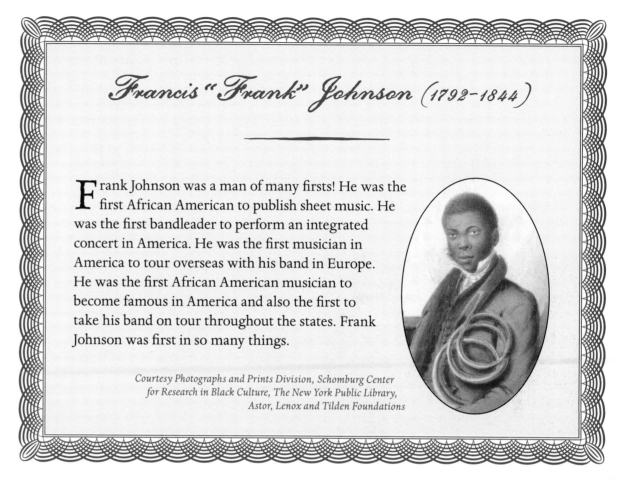

Francis "Frank" Johnson (1792–1844)

Frank Johnson was a man of many firsts! He was the first African American to publish sheet music. He was the first bandleader to perform an integrated concert in America. He was the first musician in America to tour overseas with his band in Europe. He was the first African American musician to become famous in America and also the first to take his band on tour throughout the states. Frank Johnson was first in so many things.

Courtesy Photographs and Prints Division, Schomburg Center for Research in Black Culture, The New York Public Library, Astor, Lenox and Tilden Foundations

Craft a Clay Pot

Materials

- ★ Covered worktable
- ★ Craft clay, available at craft and hobby stores
- ★ Wooden board such as an old cutting board
- ★ Rolling pin
- ★ Ruler

- ★ Paper cup or small bowl to use as pattern
- ★ Plastic knife and fork
- ★ Toothpicks
- ★ Plastic bag to store clay until project is finished

1. Prepare your worktable so it's protected. Work the clay with your hands until it is soft. Press out air bubbles.

2. Flatten a portion of the clay on the wooden board with the rolling pin until it is about ½-inch thick.

3. Using the cup or small bowl as a pattern, cut out a circle for the base of your pot with the plastic knife.

4. Use the plastic fork to lightly score, or scratch, around the edge of the flat circle.

5. Take a small ball of clay and roll it with the palms of your hands to form a long coil that resembles a snake. The coil should be about ½-inch thick.

6. Lay the coil around the edge of the flat circle to start to build the wall of the pot. Gently press on the coil to help it stick to the base of the pot.

7. Continue adding coils to the pot until it is as big as you want it.

8. Carefully use the flat edge of the plastic knife to smooth around the wall of the pot, or leave the coils as they are.

9. Use a toothpick to write your name in the clay pot, just like Dave Drake always wrote his.

10. Follow the instructions on the package of clay to dry your pot.

Famous Musician

One of the most famous artists during this era was musician and bandleader Francis "Frank" Johnson. Originally from the West Indies, Frank Johnson became one of the best-known citizens of Philadelphia. Frank Johnson owned and played a large variety of instruments. He was most famous for playing the French horn, violin, and bugle.

Frank Johnson played frequently throughout the city of Philadelphia entertaining both black and white audiences at social functions, society balls, concerts, and parades. When he was still in his 20s, he became the first African American to publish sheet music. Involved in numerous concert and military bands, Johnson soon became a leader of his own bands. During the winter, Frank Johnson's band performed locally in Philadelphia. During the summer, he traveled throughout the country performing at well-known events.

Frank Johnson set his sights on Europe. He organized and led a concert tour to play in a number of cities throughout England. He even performed before the Queen, receiving a silver bugle as a gift.

Life at Mount Vernon

George Washington's estate, Mount Vernon, was home to many enslaved African Americans. One of the most noted was William Lee, George Washington's personal valet. As Washington's attendant, Lee's duties probably included powdering the general's hair, cleaning his false teeth, and helping him dress. He was also an expert horseman. He spent many a day hunting fox or other game with Washington.

During the American Revolution, Lee was constantly at George Washington's side. By the end of the war, Lee had married. He moved back to Mount Vernon where he lived until the end of his days. In 1799, in George Washington's will, Lee was declared free and given a pension for the rest of his life. He was buried in the African burial ground at Mount Vernon.

Life at Monticello

Monticello, Thomas Jefferson's estate in Virginia, was also home to many enslaved African Americans. It took a significant number of workers to keep the gardens growing, the meals cooked, and the house well-maintained.

One of the house-servants was Sally Hemings. Family tradition as well as some historical accounts claim that Sally Hemings and Martha Jefferson were half-sisters. They had the same father but different mothers. Sally's mother was black. Martha's mother was white. Since Sally's mother was a slave, Sally was born a slave. Martha grew up and became Thomas Jefferson's wife.

When Sally and Martha's father died, infant Sally and her mother and brothers and sisters all became the property of Martha Jefferson. Their family was moved to Monticello. Some accounts say that Sally was very fair-skinned and looked a lot like her older half-sister Martha.

By the time Sally was 14, Martha Jefferson had died. Thomas Jefferson was serving in Paris as a diplomat for the United States. He requested that his daughter be sent over to Paris. Young Sally Hemings accompanied his daughter as her personal attendant.

In Paris, Sally Hemings was legally free. They did not allow slavery there. She received private lessons and circulated among the high-society circles in Paris as she accompanied Jefferson's daughter.

Monticello
Photo by author

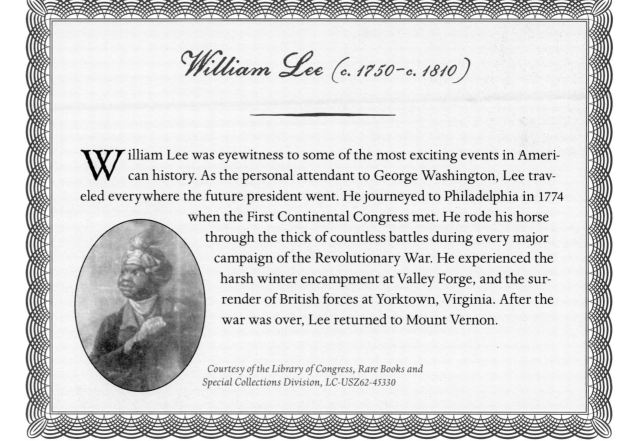

William Lee (c. 1750–c. 1810)

William Lee was eyewitness to some of the most exciting events in American history. As the personal attendant to George Washington, Lee traveled everywhere the future president went. He journeyed to Philadelphia in 1774 when the First Continental Congress met. He rode his horse through the thick of countless battles during every major campaign of the Revolutionary War. He experienced the harsh winter encampment at Valley Forge, and the surrender of British forces at Yorktown, Virginia. After the war was over, Lee returned to Mount Vernon.

Courtesy of the Library of Congress, Rare Books and Special Collections Division, LC-USZ62-45330

Andrew Bryan

Used with Permission of Documenting the American South, the University of North Carolina at Chapel Hill Libraries

Back in Monticello after Jefferson's diplomatic duties were finished in France, Sally Hemings had several children. According to the family tradition of her descendents as well as some historians, Thomas Jefferson was the father of her children. According to the law, all her children were born into slavery.

Sally Hemings's children escaped to freedom when they each were 21. Several were so fair-skinned that they chose to live as whites and keep their African American heritage a secret. Sally Hemings lived at Monticello until after the death of Thomas Jefferson. She then moved to live with her sons, Madison and Eston.

Rising Up Throughout the South

Slavery was an ugly stain on the blank pages of the newly forming nation. Its iron grip kept the southern states locked in its power, even while many of the northern states abolished slavery within their borders. Nonetheless, even throughout the South there were African American men and women who rose up with distinction to influence and shape their world.

In Savannah, Georgia, Andrew Bryan founded First African Baptist Church in 1788. Bryan started small church groups on various plantations. He preached several services each Sunday to as many as could come.

In New Orleans, James Derham established a thriving practice as a medical doctor. Originally from Philadelphia, Derham began his medical training in that city. After the American Revolution, he was sold as a medical assistant to a doctor in New Orleans, where he eventually received his freedom. Highly regarded as a professional in his field, he cared for both blacks and whites.

Marie-Thérèse Coincoin Metoyer rose to be the head of a prosperous dynasty. Originally enslaved by the founding family of Natchitoches, the earliest permanent settlement in Louisiana, she eventually was given her freedom and a plot of land. By this time, she was 40 years old and had 13 children. She built a house, started farming, and soon built a profitable plantation growing tobacco and indigo. She purchased more land as well as the freedom of many of her relatives, including her children.

Her roots and ties to her African heritage were strong. She always kept her name, Coincoin, which was African in origin. A house was built on her plantation in a unique style commonly used in Africa. Called the African House, it can still be seen today.

New Frontiers

As the newly founded nation explored new frontiers, African Americans made their mark in history.

Jean Baptiste Point Du Sable was educated in Paris before becoming a sailor. In his travels, he journeyed to New Orleans and then up to the area now called Chicago in the late 1770s, where he settled and established a prosperous trading business. He is considered the founder of Chicago.

In 1789, Olaudah Equiano, also known as Gustavus Vassa, published his autobiography. In it he tells how he was kidnapped as a child in Africa, was sold into slavery, and eventually earned his freedom. As a sailor he traveled up and down the Atlantic coast, in the West Indies, and over to England. His experiences moved him to become an outspoken abolitionist.

(left) African House
Courtesy of George Thomas Collins, great-great-great-grandson of Marie-Thérèse Coincoin Metoyer

(right) Olaudah Equiano
Courtesy of the Library Company of Philadelphia

Marie-Thérèse Coincoin Metoyer
(c. 1742–1820)

An industrious worker, shrewd businesswoman, and faithful mother, Marie-Thérèse Coincoin Metoyer established a dynasty in the region along the Cane River near Natchitoches, Louisiana. Born a slave, she bore and raised her 13 children to become prosperous landowners and influential leaders.

Receiving her freedom along with land, Marie-Thérèse Coincoin Metoyer began farming cash crops. She used her money to purchase more land and the freedom of her children. Eventually, Marie-Thérèse Coincoin Metoyer and her children became one of the wealthiest families in the nation.

Peter Williams Senior
Courtesy of the Library Company of Philadelphia

Peter Williams Junior
*Used with Permission of Documenting the American South,
the University of North Carolina at Chapel Hill Libraries*

Some of the
early church
founders were
fathers and
sons.

John Gloucester
Courtesy of the Library Company of Philadelphia

Jeremiah Gloucester
Courtesy of the Library Company of Philadelphia

New Year's Day

January 1, 1808, was a historic day in America. On this day, President Thomas Jefferson signed a bill ending the trans-Atlantic slave trade. It was a great victory. Celebrations were held. In Boston, 200 of its black citizens marched in a parade. They gathered at the African Meeting House to rejoice.

In Philadelphia, Absalom Jones delivered a powerful sermon. He urged fellow African Americans to set aside New Year's Day as a day of public thanksgiving. In the years that followed, other black preachers delivered what came to be known as "Thanksgiving Sermons" on New Year's Day. A great battle against slavery had been won.

African-American Churches

Following in the footsteps of Richard Allen and Absalom Jones, other leaders stepped forward to found churches where their members could be free to worship. In New York City, Peter Williams Sr. helped found the African Methodist Episcopal Zion Church. His son, Peter Williams Jr., helped found the Saint Phillip's African Church, also in New York City. In Philadelphia, John Gloucester started the first African American Presbyterian Church in America. His son, Jeremiah Gloucester, founded the Second African Presbyterian Church.

It was a time of growing independence from white authority within various denominations. A new day was dawning where black congregations could worship as they chose, sit where they wanted, and listen to the preachers they decided to ordain.

The War of 1812

England did not forget its former colonies, and in 1812 was back at war with the United States. When British troops attacked the capital city, many government leaders fled to the former capital, Philadelphia. By the summer of 1814, the Redcoats were on the move again. They marched out from Washington, D.C. The citizens of Philadelphia were afraid that their city would be the next battleground.

All throughout Philadelphia, men were called to arms. The city's leaders contacted Richard Allen, Absalom Jones, and James Forten. Could they organize black troops to help save the day?

They could and they did! Allen, Jones, and Forten raised 2,500 soldiers. These men worked hard alongside their fellow white citizens of Philadelphia to build earthen walls along the river to block any possible attack. Many were armed and ready to fight.

Fortunately, no attack came. The city of Philadelphia remained safe. Soon, the War of 1812 came to an end.

Founding Mothers

During the founding years of the new nation, women played an important role. Their hard work, fortitude, and willingness to fight on the home front contributed to the success and vitality of America.

One of these Founding Mothers was Sarah Bass Allen, the wife of Richard Allen. Born into slavery in Virginia, Sarah Bass came to Philadelphia while still young. She became part of Richard Allen's congregation at St. George's Methodist Episcopal Church. During the terrible Yellow Fever Epidemic of 1793, Sarah Bass served with distinction. A widow, she devoted her efforts to help families who were suffering. In his published account, Richard Allen noted her generosity and brave assistance.

Guns used by Richard Allen and black troops from Philadelphia during the War of 1812.
Courtesy of Mother Bethel AME Church

Sarah Allen (c. 1764–1849)

This Founding Mother was an inspiration to many. Working side-by-side with her husband Richard Allen, Sarah Allen helped minister to the congregation of Bethel in Philadelphia. Known affectionately as "Mother Allen," she didn't let any opportunity to help others go by. When the Yellow Fever Epidemic of 1793 swept through the city, she helped in any way she could. When young ministers arrived in tattered clothing to the first annual conference of the African Methodist Episcopal Church, she organized a sewing circle that night so the men could appear dignified at the meeting the very next day. When fugitives escaped to Philadelphia, she hid them in her home, fed and clothed them, and then sent them secretly on their way north. Strong and dignified, Sarah Allen is still admired by many today.

Courtesy of Library Company of Philadelphia

After Richard Allen's first wife Flora died, he married Sarah Bass. Together they ministered to the black community in Philadelphia. They had six children. While busy raising their children, Sarah Allen also helped purchase and manage their properties and investments.

After Bethel was founded as the mother church of the African Methodist Episcopal Church, a small group of ministers traveled to Philadelphia to attend their first annual conference. Sarah Allen knew of the great sacrifice they made ministering to congregations of slaves and free blacks. She noted the ragged condition of their clothes.

Immediately, Sarah Allen called upon the women of her congregation. A sewing society was formed to provide appropriate clothes for them to wear as leaders of the church. From that point on, the Daughters of Conference helped supply ministers with clothes and food. Women in other cities followed the example of Sarah Allen and formed similar societies.

Also a member of other societies, Sarah Allen was a leader in her community. She opened her home to church members and leaders, and also as a stop along the Underground Railroad.

A New Voice

There were not many opportunities for leadership positions to be held by women. However, a new voice was heard preaching and teaching to African Methodist Episcopal congregations. It was a voice of a woman, Jarena Lee.

Convinced that she had been called by God, Jarena Lee approached Richard Allen and explained her deep desire to preach. Because Bethel was still under the authority of St. George's Church, however, Allen could not grant her request.

Shortly after this, Lee married a pastor. They had two children, but her husband soon died. By this time, Allen had established the African Methodist Episcopal (AME) Church. He granted Lee permission to preach and hold prayer meetings.

What an amazing woman she was! At a time when African Americans held few rights, and women in general held even fewer, Lee became a powerful leader. As a woman, and especially as a black woman, her example of success inspired many. She spoke throughout Pennsylvania to various AME congregations. She traveled with Allen and other leaders to attend important church meetings.

In 1836, Lee published her autobiography, *The Life and Religious Experiences of Jarena Lee.* It is said that Sarah Allen, wishing to show her support of this remarkable woman, purchased the very first copy. The book was soon expanded and reprinted.

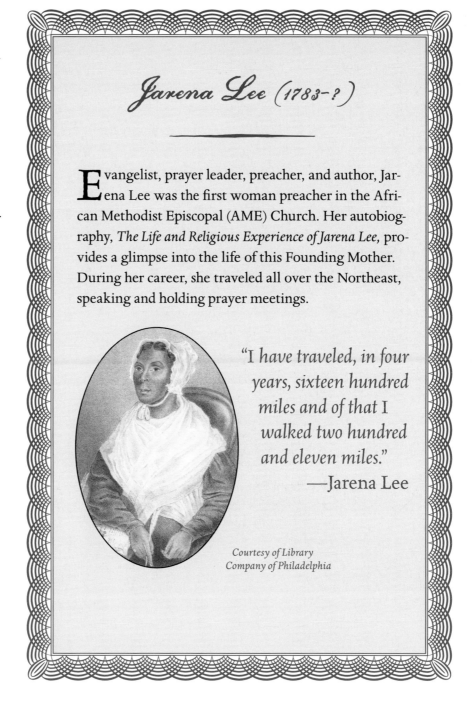

Jarena Lee (1783–?)

Evangelist, prayer leader, preacher, and author, Jarena Lee was the first woman preacher in the African Methodist Episcopal (AME) Church. Her autobiography, *The Life and Religious Experience of Jarena Lee,* provides a glimpse into the life of this Founding Mother. During her career, she traveled all over the Northeast, speaking and holding prayer meetings.

"I have traveled, in four years, sixteen hundred miles and of that I walked two hundred and eleven miles."
—Jarena Lee

Courtesy of Library Company of Philadelphia

Industrious Businesswoman

Another woman who published a book during this era was Elleanor Eldridge. A hard-working woman, her memoirs detail the story of her struggles and success. In the *Memoirs of Elleanor Eldridge*, readers learned of her work ethic. Eldridge worked as a housemaid, a whitewasher, and a laundress. She wisely saved her earnings and purchased land and buildings from her income.

Elleanor Eldridge

Used with Permission of Documenting the American South, the University of North Carolina at Chapel Hill Libraries

At the height of her financial success, however, she became the victim of fraud. When others illegally attempted to overtake her properties, she rallied the support of her community to purchase her book. She raised enough money to gain back everything she had lost.

Eldridge's success as a self-made working-woman is an inspirational example. Even in the face of adversity, she overcame her trials. In an era when the black working class was thought of with little regard, she showed the world that African American women took pride in their work.

New Black Societies

From the late 1700s to the mid-1800s, various societies flourished within free black communities. Women formed many female literary societies, anti-slavery societies, and benevolent societies. Led by Richard Allen, Absalom Jones, and James Forten, the large African American community in Philadelphia was the first to establish many societies. Most societies of this era had a three-fold goal: self-improvement, abolition of slavery, and assistance to those in need.

Temperance societies were formed where members pledged to stay away from alcoholic drinks. Bible societies were formed where the foundations of Scripture were taught. Welfare and benevolent societies were formed to help provide assistance to widows, orphans, or those too sick to work. Educational societies were formed to promote learning among its adult members as well as provide equal educational opportunities.

Numerous literary societies were also formed. William Whipper, a leading black abolitionist in Philadelphia, helped found a literary society. The goal of Philadelphia's Reading Society was to establish a library and to hold meetings to discuss books members had read. Whipper was a frequent speaker at various literary societies, encouraging members everywhere to be well-read.

The Fight for Equal Education

In the early 1800s, the Augustine Society was founded in Philadelphia. Richard Allen, Absalom Jones, James Forten, and John Gloucester were among its founding members. Determined to provide an equal education for children of African American families, the Augustine Society opened its own school. Similar societies were soon formed in other cities. Schools were opened and teachers were hired to provide African American children a solid education where previously there had been none available.

Educator and abolitionist Prince Saunders spoke before the Augustine Society in 1818. Delivering his speech at Bethel, Saunders proclaimed to his listeners the importance of

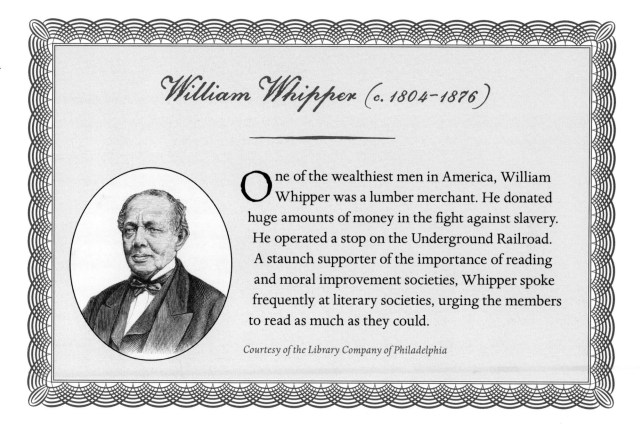

William Whipper (c. 1804-1876)

One of the wealthiest men in America, William Whipper was a lumber merchant. He donated huge amounts of money in the fight against slavery. He operated a stop on the Underground Railroad. A staunch supporter of the importance of reading and moral improvement societies, Whipper spoke frequently at literary societies, urging the members to read as much as they could.

Courtesy of the Library Company of Philadelphia

"The hope is encouraged that you will never be weary in labouring for the promotion of the cause and interests of science and literature among the rising generation of the people of colour."

—Prince Saunders

educating African American youth. Prince Saunders had himself been educated at schools in Vermont and Connecticut. After attending college, he became a teacher at Boston's African School and was involved with various literary and benevolent societies. Saunders was highly admired for his eloquence and leadership abilities.

The Sunday School Movement

During the founding years of the United States of America, children of the nation's poor often suffered from a lack of educational opportunity. Catherine "Katy" Ferguson of New York City stepped forward to help. Known as the founder of the first Sunday school in New York City, Ferguson had herself been raised in near-poverty conditions. She was born on a schooner while her enslaved mother was traveling to New York. Separated as a child from her only known family member when her mother was sold away, Ferguson felt compassion for motherless children and reached out to care for them the remainder of her days.

While a teenager, Ferguson purchased her freedom, half from her own wages and half from donations by local abolitionists. She married at the young age of 18. Tragically, however, the two infants she had both died. Her husband died soon after.

She was more determined than ever to help the poor and the motherless. Visiting the local almshouse, or poorhouse, as well as local impoverished neighborhoods in New York City, Ferguson gathered nearly 50 children each week to attend an integrated school in her home on Sunday mornings. At her Sunday school, she gave the children spiritual guidance as well as academic instruction even though she herself never learned to read or write. Everything she taught was based on what she had memorized from hearing others teach. During the rest of the week, she established a successful career as caterer of baked goods.

When the minister at the church she attended heard what she was doing on Sundays, he visited her school. Amazed at all she was accomplishing for the city's neglected

Form a a Literary Society

Celebrate the love of reading by forming a literary society. Plan a regular meeting day and time to meet. Find a place to meet that suits your needs. If this is a private society, it can meet in your backyard. If it's a public society, it can meet in an empty classroom at school.

Discuss the guidelines for your society. Do you want all members to read the same book and meet to discuss it? Do you want to offer a variety of activities during your meetings such as movies, games, or guest speakers? Do you want to work together on a community service project such as donating new books to a children's shelter? Elect officers to organize and run the society, or simply appoint one person to lead each meeting. Write down the guidelines you decide to follow and give every member a copy.

Catherine Ferguson
(c. 1774–1854)

Catherine "Katy" Ferguson last saw her own mother when she was young. After Catherine was tragically torn from her arms, her mother was sold. As an adult, this memory compelled her to reach out and help neglected children from the poor neighborhoods of New York City. She established an integrated Sunday school. Spanning a successful career of over 40 years, Catherine Ferguson is remembered as the founder of the first Sunday school in New York City.

Used with Permission of Documenting the American South, the University of North Carolina at Chapel Hill Libraries

Daniel Coker
Courtesy of the Library Company of Philadelphia

children, the minister invited Ferguson to move her school to the church. Assistants were provided to teach with her.

For the next 40 years, Catherine Ferguson oversaw the integrated Sunday school. This Founding Mother cared for her students, provided food for them, and often found them families where they could grow up to live a happier life. Many of the children she took into her own home and raised herself.

The Birth of a Denomination

During the early 1800s, many great trials and hardships were experienced by Richard Allen and other leaders of black congregations. Racist white church leaders determined to take charge of these religious gatherings of free blacks operating underneath the authority of their denominations. Other white citizens rallied, however, to support Allen and his fellow African American church leaders. It was a trying time. Yet it had its triumphs.

Allen and other church leaders such as Daniel Coker of Baltimore decided to establish a new denomination. In April 1816, Allen made a daring move. Communicating with local ministers in Philadelphia as well as leaders of black congregations in other cities, he called them to assemble in a conference at Bethel.

At least 16 church leaders gathered at this first conference to discuss the conditions of the church. Allen was elected to preside as chairman over the meeting with Coker elected vice-chairman. Richard Allen Jr., then only 14 years old, acted as secretary of the meeting.

It was a time to organize. Numerous small churches had sprung up in the shadow of Bethel. What was to become of them?

There were no denominations for African American churches, and each African American congregation was under white authority. Why should black churches have to function under the decisions of white leaders when black leaders were capable of leading their own congregations?

Even though the trans-Atlantic slave trade had been outlawed in 1808, slavery was still an established institution. How could African Americans lead the fight for civil rights if they only had limited freedom in their own churches—the main religious, social, and political organizations of that era?

"As for Richard Allen, the time will come, when all Christian men, whether white or black, who love the Lord Jesus, will recognize in him one of the greatest philanthropists of his times."
—George F. Bragg

Early ballot box used to elect church officials. Images representing candidates were placed in the top slots. Black or white marbles were placed in the corresponding hole to indicate a yes or no vote.

Courtesy of Mother Bethel AME Church

(top) Historic building of Mt. Pisgah AME Church in Everett, Pennsylvania.

(bottom) Mt. Pisgah AME Zion Church in Bedford, Pennsylvania.

Photos courtesy of Jacksons Journeys

> "We deemed it expedient to have a form of discipline, whereby we may guide our people in the fear of God, in the unity of the Spirit, and in the bonds of peace, and preserve us from that spiritual despotism which we have so recently experienced."
>
> —Richard Allen

Being both the pioneer and the great organizer that he was, Richard Allen once again forged the way. During the conference, it was determined that a new denomination would be formed, the African Methodist Episcopal (AME) Church. Its leaders, its ministers, and even its bishop would be African American. Nothing like this had ever existed before.

At first, the young and enthusiastic Daniel Coker was elected as bishop. He politely declined. Then the much older Richard Allen was chosen. He graciously accepted. Allen became the first bishop of the first black denomination in the nation.

As bishop, his duties would be far and wide. He would found churches. He would build a network of support. He would organize and hold yearly conferences. He would work tirelessly at the humongous task of overseeing the growth of what would one day be one of the largest denominations in the country.

But not yet. Those duties were still to come. For now, a more urgent need arose. Just months after founding the African Methodist Episcopal Church, Allen found himself facing another giant: the newly formed American Colonization Society.

Anti-Colonization

In December of 1816, the American Colonization Society was formed. Its goal was to transport free blacks to the shores of Africa as pioneers to establish settlements. It was backed by presidents and government officials, with most of its leaders coming from the South. Many of them were slaveholders. The

> *"They declared that they had been among the first to come to America and that they would not voluntarily leave their country."*
> —Charles H. Wesley

American Colonization Society caused a tremendous stir.

At first, leaders of free black communities thought a back-to-Africa movement might be beneficial. Establishing a new settlement in Africa where everyone could experience equal rights without the harsh consequences of racism sounded appealing.

As more and more information was presented to the public, however, Richard Allen, James Forten, and the majority of the free black population grew to feel that the American Colonization Society was in actuality a plot to make slavery an even stronger institution than it already was. By removing free blacks from America—citizens who could vote in support of equal rights, send petitions to the government demanding equal rights, and help those who were in bondage—African

> *"We ask not their compassion and aid, in assisting us to emigrate to Africa, we are contented in the land that gave us birth, and which many of us fought for, and many of our Fathers fought and died for, during the war which established our independence."*
> —James Forten

Americans who were enslaved would lose the strongest advocates they had.

An urgent mass meeting was held at Bethel in Philadelphia in January of 1817. Over 3,000 African American citizens attended. Similar meetings were held in other major cities such as Boston and New York. In one accord, their strong voices united and cried out, "We will not abandon our brethren in chains!"

Back-to-Africa

This was not the first time a back-to-Africa movement had been proposed. Wealthy merchant and sailor Paul Cuffe was one of its earliest advocates. Traveling up and down the Atlantic seaboard, Cuffe developed a plan to transport freed slaves back to Africa. Once there, they would grow crops and produce goods to trade with England and America based on arrangements and investments that would provide a profit for former slave owners. By establishing an alternate profit from cash crops and manufactured goods, Cuffe hoped to bring an end to slavery.

In 1811, Cuffe left Philadelphia and sailed to Sierra Leone in Africa. He planned to sail each year to Sierra Leone with new settlers of freed slaves from America. His goal was to then sail back to America with a shipload of products to trade. The War of 1812 interrupted his plans.

In 1815, Cuffe sailed on his first official back-to-Africa voyage. He transported nearly 40 African Americans on his ship to settle in Sierra Leone. Soon after this, however, Cuffe became ill. He battled with illness for a time, then died in 1817. Just as the American Colonization Society was gaining momentum, Paul Cuffe's own plans came to an end.

Black Abolitionists

With the rise of the American Colonization Society, free blacks united to protest its agenda. In 1826 another mass meeting was held in Philadelphia. James Forten and Jeremiah Gloucester were the leaders of the day.

> "We will never separate ourselves voluntarily from the slave population in this country; they are our brethren by ties of consanguinity, of suffering, and of wrong, and we feel that there is more virtue in suffering privations with them, than fancied advantage for a season."
>
> —James Forten

Paul Cuffe (Also known as Cuffee) (1759–1817)

Paul Cuffe's father was originally from the west coast of Africa. His mother was a Wampanoag from North America. Proud of both his African and Native American heritage, Cuffe grew up with a love of the sea. He worked hard on whalers sailing up and down the Atlantic coast. During the American Revolution he was captured by the British and imprisoned on a prison ship. After the war he went on to become a wealthy merchant and captain of his own vessel. A founder of the back-to-Africa movement, Cuffe's intent was to help bring an end to slavery by establishing a successful trading enterprise with freed slaves relocated in Sierra Leone. Dying from illness at an early age, however, he left his great fortune to his children. His daughters became two of the few women in the country to own a ship, and his descendents became well-known merchant mariners as well as staunch abolitionists.

Silhouette of Paul Cuffe
Courtesy of the Library of Congress, Prints & Photographs Division, LC-USZ62-26174

129

(above) Sojourner Truth
Courtesy of the Library of Congress, Prints & Photographs Division, LC-USZ62-119343

(right) John Russwurm
Courtesy of the Library Company of Philadelphia

> *"We wish to plead our own cause. Too long have others spoken for us."*
> —John Russwurm

It was during this time that a new group of leaders stepped forward. Some were the same Black Founders, such as Richard Allen and James Forten of Philadelphia and George Middleton of Boston, but others were from the new generation. Together, these black abolitionists spoke frequently and passionately about the evils of slavery. They funded, founded, and led anti-slavery organizations.

John Russwurm and Samuel Cornish published the *Freedom's Journal*, the first newspaper owned and written by African Americans. Many articles from leading black abolitionists were published in it, including letters written by James Forten attacking the American Colonization Society. Another new antislavery organization was the Free Produce Society. The members of this society bought items raised only on farms where African American workers were hired as free citizens. In addition to these groups, speakers such as Sojourner Truth and Frederick Douglass traveled from town to town, raising public awareness about slavery.

Word traveled deep into the South that the fight for freedom was growing strong. Some of those who were enslaved escaped. Finding their way along secret routes known today as the Underground Railroad, many received food, clothing, and travel accommodations. Slave revolts led by such leaders as Nat Turner and Joseph Cinqué rocked the nation. It was a time of turmoil and fear, as well as strength and heroism.

The first and only successful slave revolt was led by a man known as Joseph Cinqué. Born Sengbe Pieh, he was kidnapped near his home in Sierra Leone and sold to a slave ship sailing to Cuba. Surviving the horrible Middle Passage, he was given the new Spanish name Joseph Cinqué.

Put aboard a ship once more with about 40 other kidnapped Africans, they set sail on

Publish a Newspaper

Freedom's Journal was a newspaper read by many abolitionists. You can publish your own newspaper, too.

Materials

★ Sample issues of various newspapers

★ Writing supplies

★ Digital camera (optional)

1. Decide on a purpose for your newspaper. Do you want it to focus on one theme or be about a variety of things?

2. Look at the front pages of the newspaper samples you collected. What do you notice? Choose a title for your newspaper, and design the layout of the title to look similar to the newspaper samples you've read.

3. Explore the newspaper samples to discover different sections a newspaper can contain. Which sections do you want your newspaper to have?

4. Be a reporter! Interview people to find more information for your articles. Ask questions such as who, what, when, where, why, and how? Take pictures of people, places, and special events to include in your features.

5. Write your articles to fit into narrow columns, just like a real newspaper.

6. Photocopy it and share it with family and friends.

Joseph Cinqué
(Also known as Cinquez)
(c. 1814–c. 1879)

Born in Sierra Leone, Africa, Sengbe Pieh was kidnapped from his home. Chained below deck in a slave ship, he was taken across the Atlantic Ocean to Cuba. By now he had been given the Spanish name Joseph Cinqué. On board a second ship sailing to his new owner's plantation, Cinqué organized and led the first and only successful slave revolt in American history.

After overtaking the ship, he commanded the remaining white men on board to sail back to Africa during the day. During the night, however, the slavers tricked the Africans by sailing northwest. Eventually, the ship landed near Long Island, New York. Cinqué and the other Africans on board were put in jail. The court listened to their appeals for freedom from slavery, and the Africans were set free.

Cinqué and the others joined a boat of missionaries returning to Sierra Leone. The journey was successful, and the amazing story of Joseph Cinqué became an inspiration to all.

Courtesy of the Library Company of Philadelphia

the *Amistad* for their new owner's plantation. By this time, Cinqué decided to take matters into his own hands. He picked the lock on his chains with a nail, freed himself and his fellow Africans, and took over the ship.

Once Cinqué was in command, he ordered the white slavers to sail the ship back to Africa toward the rising sun. During the night, however, the slavers headed north instead, hoping to land in the southern United States. To everyone's surprise, they landed near Long Island, New York.

The slavers immediately insisted that the Africans were their property and must be returned to Cuba. Cinqué and the other Africans were put in prison while their trial went to court. Supported by leading abolitionists of the day, Cinqué told the horrible story in court about being kidnapped into slavery. Former president and staunch abolitionist John Quincy Adams represented their case—and they won! The Africans were set free.

> "We may as well die in trying to be free as be killed and eaten."
> —Joseph Cinqué

The National Convention Movement

Already a leader and organizer, Richard Allen continued to forge the way. When asked about the possibility of forming a national convention of support and networking for African Americans throughout the nation, Allen determined to take action.

Immediate plans followed. Allen contacted Black Founders in other cities. A date was set—September 15, 1830—and a place was chosen—Bethel Church in Philadelphia.

Bishop Richard Allen was elected president and William Whipper the secretary. Forty delegates arrived at Bethel for the first national convention. They represented churches in seven states. More would have come except for the fact that recent laws restricted free blacks from traveling freely.

These restrictions of freedom were some of the issues that were discussed. The delegates organized a nationwide network of support. They united against the American Colonization Society.

> *"Never have any people in proportion to their means of operation, made greater efforts for their entire enfranchisement."*
> —Joseph Willson

> *"Since the period of the meeting of the first Convention—though only 10 years—the condition of the people of color has undergone a great and beneficial change."*
> —Joseph Willson

The name these members chose for their first national convention was the American Society of Free Persons of Colour. A constitution was written up based on the principles outlined in the Declaration of Independence.

Plans were made to meet again the next year. The delegates returned home. Their course was set to unite African Americans in the fight for civil rights.

What thoughts went through Richard Allen's mind as he returned home? He was now 70 years old. He had lived a long and very successful life. Against all odds, he had thrown off the chains of slavery and declared himself a free man. He had struggled against persecution to become one of the new nation's Black Founders. He had accomplished many firsts and established numerous important institutions. He had fought the good fight. Now he was leading the fight once again.

Richard Allen
Courtesy of the Library Company of Philadelphia

But not for much longer. Richard Allen became sick and died on March 26, 1831. A monumental life came to an end.

His legacy did not end, however. His great work continued. Other leaders stepped forward in the march toward freedom and civil rights. A new holiday, Richard Allen Day, was established. The National Convention Movement lasted over the next decade. African Americans throughout the nation connected with each other. Together, they united with one voice that carried far into the future for new generations to hear, "Freedom and liberty for all!"

Entrance to Richard Allen's tomb in the Richard Allen Museum, Philadelphia, Pennsylvania.
Courtesy of Mother Bethel AME Church

Afterword

America's Black Founders helped build a nation that would become one of the most influential countries in the world. Even though many traditional history books have been silent concerning the important contributions and accomplishments of African Americans during the founding of the nation, America's Black Founders were not silent. Even though nearly all doors were closed to the presence of African Americans during this era, they made their presence known. Through the petitions they wrote, the sermons they preached, the literature they published, the churches they built, and the organizations they formed, African Americans influenced the birth of a new nation in powerful and far-reaching ways.

Their story is our story. Their history is our history. From the first settlement in Jamestown to the first battle of the Revolutionary War, African Americans were active participants in the founding of America. In every major engagement of the American Revolution, black patriots fought, often with distinction. From the seedbeds of revolution in Boston to the establishment of the nation's first capital in Philadelphia, they helped forge the way through the strong leadership of such greats as Richard Allen, Absalom Jones, James Forten, and Prince Hall.

State by state, these individuals' powerful voices and dedicated pursuit of equal rights brought about emancipation throughout the North. Month by month and year by year, they fought with focused determination for freedoms and liberties until the trans-Atlantic slave trade finally came to an end. Their generation influenced a new generation of freedom fighters and black abolitionists whose ceaseless efforts helped bring an end to slavery through the Civil War. The nation's first civil rights leaders set the stage for the leaders of the civil rights movement more than a century later. The powerful voices of America's Black Founders still ring loud and clear to inspire future generations of Americans.

Resources

WEB SITES TO EXPLORE

African American Odyssey: Free Blacks in the Antebellum Period
http://memory.loc.gov/ammem/aaohtml/exhibit/aopart2b.html#0205
This site features primary source documents such as Revolutionary War documents of black patriots as well as a short overview from the American Revolution to the Civil War.

Africans in America: America's Journey Through Slavery
www.pbs.org/wgbh/aia/
This educational site corresponds with the public television documentary. Original documents, paintings, and images bring African American history to life from 1450 to 1865. Lists of resources and teacher's guides are included.

Black Heritage Trail
www.afroammuseum.org/index.htm
View the online tour of the Black Heritage Trail in Boston. This site also celebrates key moments in African American history that took place in Boston.

The Black Past: Remembered and Reclaimed
http://blackpast.org
This site is dedicated to providing reference materials on African American history. It features speeches, articles, encyclopedia entries, and links to other Web sites highlighting important events and personalities.

African Americans and the End of Slavery in Massachusetts
By the Massachusetts Historical Society
www.masshist.org/endofslavery
Containing a large database of artifacts and original documents, this site provides a variety of information and images. See Phillis Wheatley's desk, read petitions for freedom, look at the Bucks of America medallion, and more!

Mother Bethel AME Church
www.motherbethel.org
Learn more about Richard Allen and the history of the AME Church by exploring this Web site. Follow the links to visit the online home of the Richard Allen museum.

Schomburg Center for Research in Black Culture
www.nypl.org/research/sc/sc.html
Explore the online exhibits, collections, and digital images on this important site. It is also a great place for research and to find information on other available resources.

Wallbuilders: African American History Resources
http://wallbuilders.com/LIBissuesArticles.asp?id=88
This site is dedicated to educating the public about America's nearly forgotten past surrounding the founding years of our nation, with an emphasis on our moral, religious, and constitutional heritage. It has articles, links, and products that focus on the important role African Americans had in the founding of America.

SELECTED BIBLIOGRAPHY

Alexander, E. Curtis. *Richard Allen.* New York: ECA Associates, 1985.

Bennett, Lerone, Jr. *Before the Mayflower.* New York: Penguin Books, 1988.

Blockson, Charles L. *African Americans in Pennsylvania: Above Ground and Underground.* Harrisburg, Pennsylvania: RB Books, 2001.

Blockson, Charles L. *The Liberty Bell Era.* Harrisburg: RB Books, 2003.

Bolster, W. Jeffrey. *Black Jacks: African American Seamen in the Age of Sail.* Cambridge, Massachusetts: Harvard University Press, 1997.

Carretta, Vincent, Ed. *Phillis Wheatley: Complete Writings.* New York: Penguin Books, 2001.

Cox, Clinton. *Come All You Brave Soldiers: Blacks in the Revolutionary War.* New York: Scholastic, Inc., 2002.

Dorman, Franklin A. *Twenty Families of Color in Massachusetts.* Boston: New England Historic Genealogical Society, 1998.

Gates, Henry Louis Gates Jr. and Evelyn Brooks Higginbotham. *African American National Biography.* New York: Oxford University Press, 2008.

George, Carol V.R. *Segregated Sabbaths.* New York: Oxford University Press, 1973.

Hine, Darlene Clark. *Black Women in America: An Historical Encyclopedia.* Brooklyn, New York: Carlson Publishing Inc., 1993.

Kaplan, Sidney and Emma Nogrady Kaplan. *The Black Presence in the Era of the American Revolution.* Amherst: The University of Massachusetts Press, 1989.

Mathews, Marcia M. *Richard Allen.* Baltimore: Helicon, 1963.

McKissack, Patricia C. and Fredrick L. McKissack. *Black Hands, White Sails: The Story of African-American Whalers.* New York: Scholastic, 1999.

Nash, Gary B. *Forging Freedom.* Cambridge, Massachusetts: Harvard University Press, 1988.

Nell, William C. *Colored Patriots of the American Revolution.* Salem, New Hampshire: Ayer Company, 1986.

Newman, Richard S. *Freedom's Prophet: Bishop Richard Allen, the AME Church, and the Black Founding Fathers.* New York: New York University Press, 2008.

Newman, Richard, Patrick Rael, and Phillip Lapsansky, Ed. *Pamphlets of Protest.* New York: Routledge, 2001.

Porter, Dorothy. *Early Negro Writing: 1760–1837.* Boston: Beacon Press, 1971.

Quarles, Benjamin. *The Negro in the American Revolution.* New York: W. W. Norton & Company, 1961.

Smith, Jessie Carney. *Black Firsts.* Detroit: Visible Ink Press, 1994.

Smith, Jessie Carney. *Notable Black American Men.* Detroit, Michigan: Gale Group, 1999.

Smith, Jessie Carney. *Notable Black American Women.* Detroit, Michigan: Gale Group, 1992.

Sterling, Dorothy. *Speak Out in Thunder Tones: Letters and Other Writings by Black Northerners, 1787–1865.* New York: Doubleday, 1973.

Wesley, Charles H. *Richard Allen: Apostle of Freedom.* Washington, D. C.: The Associated Publishers, 1969.

Winch, Julie. *A Gentleman of Color: The Life of James Forten.* New York: Oxford University Press, 2002.

ALSO FOR STUDENTS

Baker, Charles F., Ed. *Footsteps: African American History: Sally Hemings.* Peterborough, New Hampshire: Cobblestone Publishing Company, 1999.

Diamond, Arthur. *Prince Hall.* Philadelphia: Chelsea House Publishers, 1992.

Klots, Steve. *Richard Allen.* New York: Chelsea House Publishers, 1991.

Nordquist, Marty, Ed. *Voices in African American History: The American Revolution.* Cleveland, Ohio: Modern Curriculum Press, 1994.

Pinkney, Andrea Davis. *Dear Benjamin Banneker.* New York: Harcourt Brace, 1994.

Raatma, Lucia. *African-American Soldiers in the American Revolution.* Minneapolis, Minnesota: Compass Point Books, 2008.

Sanders, Nancy I. *A Kid's Guide to African American History.* Chicago: Chicago Review Press, 2007.

————. *D Is for Drinking Gourd: An African American Alphabet*, illustrated by E. B. Lewis. Chelsea, MI: Sleeping Bear Press, 2007.

————. *Readers Theatre for African American History.* Santa Barbara, CA: Libraries Unlimited, 2008.

Index

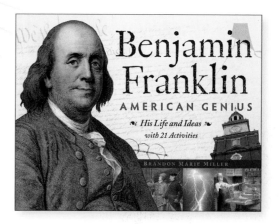

The American Revolution for Kids

A History with 21 Activities
By Janis Herbert

Ages 9 & up

Two-color interior, photos and
illustrations throughout

A Smithsonian Notable Book for Children

*"The dramatic events that lay behind the
Founding Fathers' struggle for liberty are
vividly recounted in Herbert's lively survey."*

—*Smithsonian*

The true accounts of those who created the
United States come to life in this activity
book celebrating freedom and democracy.

ISBN 978-1-55652-456-1 · $16.95 (CAN $18.95)

e-book: 978-1-55652-841-5, $11.95

George Washington for Kids

His Life and Times with 21 Activities
By Brandon Marie Miller

Ages 9 & up

Two-color interior, photos and
illustrations throughout

George Washington comes alive in this fascinating activity book that introduces the
leader to whom citizens turned again and
again—to lead them through eight long
years of war, to guide them as they wrote
a new Constitution, and to act as the new
nation's first executive leader.

ISBN 978-1-55652-655-8 · $14.95 (CAN $18.95)

e-book: 978-1-55652-836-1, $11.95

Benjamin Franklin, American Genius

His Life and Ideas with 21 Activities
By Brandon Marie Miller

Ages 9 & up

Two-color interior, photos and
illustrations throughout

*"This smart and delightful book
captures the magic of Benjamin Franklin
and shows why his life is so inspiring.
Above all, it celebrates his creativity,
which was the source of his genius."*

—Walter Isaacson, author of
Benjamin Franklin: An American Life

ISBN 978-1-55652-757-9 · $16.95 (CAN $18.95)

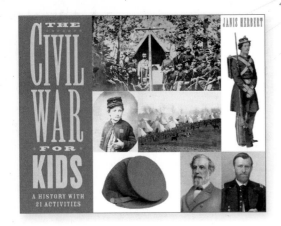

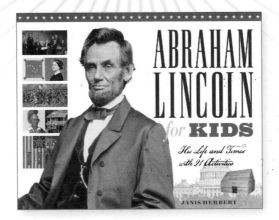

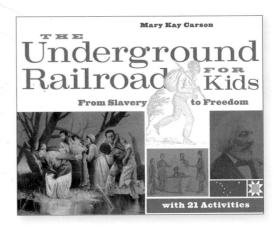

The Civil War for Kids

A History with 21 Activities
By Janis Herbert

Ages 9 & up

Two-color interior, photos throughout

"For children who really want to know what it felt like to take an active role in the past, The Civil War for Kids is it!"

—Civil War Book Review

ISBN 978-1-55652-355-7 · $16.95 (CAN $18.95)

Abraham Lincoln for Kids

His Life and Times with 21 Activities
By Janis Herbert

Ages 9 & up

Two-color interior, photos throughout

"This original, informative, and entertaining book . . . should be required reading for every young person seeking a vivid introduction to Lincoln's life."

—Harold Holzer, cochairman,
U.S. Lincoln Bicentennial Commission

ISBN 978-1-55652-656-5 · $16.95 (CAN $18.95)

e-book: 978-1-55652-830-9, $11.95

The Underground Railroad for Kids

From Slavery to Freedom with 21 Activities
By Mary Kay Carson

Ages 9 & up

Two-color interior, photos and illustrations throughout

"Mixes history with craft and do-it-yourself projects to bring the past to life."

—The Buffalo News

ISBN 978-1-55652-554-4 · $16.95 (CAN $18.95)

e-book: 978-1-55652-628-2, $12.50